STILE FLOREALE

Edited by Nancy Eickel

Designed by
Jacques Auger Design Associates, Inc.

Front and back cover:
Galileo Chini. Glazed earthenware tile,
ca. 1898-99. Cat. no. 27.

ISBN: 0-295-96671-8 (cloth)
ISBN: 0-295-96670-X (paper)

Library of Congress Cataloging-in-Publication
Data

Weisberg, Gabriel P.
   The stile floreale: the cult of nature in Italian
   design / by Gabriel P. Weisberg.

   p.   cm.
   Bibliography: p. 125
   Includes index.
   1. Decoration and ornament – Plant forms –
Italy – History – 19th century – Exhibitions.
2. Decoration and ornament – Plant forms –
Italy – History – 20th century – Exhibitions.
3. Mitchell Wofson Jr. Collection of Decorative
and Propaganda Arts – Exhibitions.
I. Title.
NK1452.A1W45 1988
745.4′4945-dc19   88-3645
                                     CIP

Photography credits:
Stuart Friedman: illus. 2; figs. 2, 14, 15
Howard Goodman: fig. 7
Library of Congress: figs. 23-26
Metropolitan Museum of Art: fig. 22
Giustino Rampazzi: illus. 3, 4; figs. 18-21
G. P. Weisberg: figs. 5, 8
W.W. Willard Associates: illus. 1; figs. 1, 3, 4, 6,
   9-13, 16, 17, 27-30, 34-114

STILE FLOREALE:
THE CULT OF NATURE IN ITALIAN DESIGN

BY GABRIEL P. WEISBERG

THE WOLFSONIAN FOUNDATION
MIAMI, FLORIDA

TABLE OF CONTENTS

DEDICATED TO THE MEMORY OF AGOSTINO LAURO.

PREFACE

The first exhibition of the Italian "Liberty" style opened in Milan in December of 1972. A few months earlier, at the Centro Pirelli, there was an exhibition of architectural drawings from the municipal building files. These activities drew attention and lent credibility to the first studies of "modernism made in Italy," which were done in the sixties. At the time, Europe and the United States renewed their interest in those artists discussed by Nikolaus Pevsner in his celebrated book, *Pioneers of the Modern Movement,* 1936.

While exhibitions and publications were abundant, there was very little written about the Italian production during the Art Nouveau period. Even when mention was made, no significant information was forthcoming with the exception of *L'Art de 1900 ou le Style Jules Verne,* Paris, 1965.

It would be unfair to fault foreign scholars and critics for this omission, even though Italian modernists had exhibited their work and won awards in international expositions. The omission was mostly the fault of Italy itself, which during the time gave little recognition to a period of its own artistic culture, even though it had seen the creation of intelligent and exquisite works mirroring international taste. It was a period which had also provided a series of craftsmen of major importance from various fields, including woodwork, metalwork, and glasswork, who evolved due to their existence in a country rich in craft traditions.

It is an unfortunate paradox that Italy, of all places, did not pursue the study and appreciation of the statement made at the Turin exposition of 1902. Therefore, the exhibition *Stile Floreale: The Cult of Nature in Italian Design* and its accompanying catalogue focus much deserved attention on Italy at the turn of the century.

The 1960s saw the beginning of some of these explorations with such publications as Valentino Brosio's *Lo Stile Liberty in Italia,* Milan, 1967, and my first book *Il Liberty in Italia,* Milan, 1968; the catalogue of the 1972 Milan exhibition referred to earlier; and *L'Italia Liberty,* Milan, 1973 authored by Bairati, Bossaglia, and Rosci. From this time on, the literature regarding Liberty is abundant, as this catalogue shows. The most recent publication to join this bibliography is my last work, *Archivi del Liberty Italiano: Architettura,* Milan, 1988.

Regardless of this, the research on this rich and articulated phenomenon may still bring interesting surprises and discoveries. This is especially true in regard to artistic production at the turn of the century or before the rise of the Wiener Secession, whose characteristics represent naturalistic (even though stylized) features, including floral and vegetal morphology, justifying the success of the "stile floreale" expression.

In Italy, both Italian and foreign production were generally called "Liberty" after the well-known London house. But the name Stile Floreale was preferred by many, giving a continuity to the Italian tradition from the Renaissance to Modernism. In 1902, the thirteenth-century expression *dolce stil novo* was applied by some writers to Italian decorative art of the floral style, thus revealing the connection between Stile Floreale and the poetic pre-Raphaelites.

It seems to me of historical significance and of refined interpretation that this exhibition held in America, being among the few exhibitions outside of Italy to concentrate on the specific theme of the Italian "Liberty" style, should designate it the Stile Floreale.

Rossana Bossaglia
Milan

FOREWORD

The line between art and craft has never been easy to determine. This controversial issue generated much debate in Europe and the United States at the turn of the century, when the art nouveau movement intensified many questions about the nature of art and design, and in particular, the place of technology in a world striving to achieve creative fulfillment. Today, Italian design undisputedly ranks as an important facet of international artistic life, yet Italy has not always played such a preeminent role. In large part, *Stile Floreale: The Cult of Nature in Italian Design* traces one aspect of Italy's emergence as a leading participant in contemporary architectural and interior design.

When the First International Exposition of Modern Decorative Art opened in Turin in 1902, Italy was generally considered a fragmented participant in the evolution of European design. It was seen as a nation not yet fully sympathetic to art nouveau and the design reform movement then sweeping the continent. After all, France, Germany, and Belgium (illus. 1) as well as the distinct artistic identities of England and Scotland were all making significant contributions to the development of a ``new style.'' This spirit of international achievement in the decorative arts, and the influence the fine arts could exert over design, were emphasized throughout the Turin exposition, as a section of the German pavilion by Peter Behrens so aptly proved (illus. 2). By 1902, however, Italy still struggled to catch up and to attain its own stylistic advances. Even though it was held relatively late in the art nouveau period, the Turin exposition was in essence Italy's bid for recognition and legitimacy in European design.

Turin's selection as the site for this grand display of modern decorative art was based upon its impressive history as an art center and a city open to diverse stylistic trends, especially those in architecture. In Turin, the exposition's organizers were also assured of a receptive audience, one composed in part of wealthy industrialists and entrepreneurs eager to support innovations in Italian design. The resulting exposition, although viewed by a few as art nouveau's last major showcase, was welcomed by others as proof of the possible cooperation of art and industry. Designers now were seen as incorporating technological progress into their creations. Distinctions between artists and craftsmen blurred as architectural and interior designers assumed greater influence in shaping the modern decorative arts.

Now, more than eighty-five years after the First International Exposition of Modern Decorative Art closed, we once again have the opportunity to discover some of the objects, visually unified room installations, and imaginative architectural details unveiled at Turin. With this comes the chance to examine objectively the legacy of the Turin exposition of 1902 and to place modern design in historical context. Perhaps a most inspiring and appropriate starting point for this investigation into Italian design is Agostino Lauro, a distinguished furniture maker (illus. 3) who created for his country's section of the Turin exposition a highly praised palazzina.

3 Plaque commemorating Agostino Lauro at the School of Professional Upholstery and Decorating in Turin. It reads: 27 February 1861 – 3 November 1924. In honor of the everlasting memory of Agostino Lauro. Creator and master of high artistic achievement. May his memory lend support to the work, merit and dignity of those who follow his art. (See note 43.)

Indeed, it was extremely fortunate that Mitchell Wolfson, Jr., founder of The Wolfsonian Foundation, purchased a complete "double parlor" designed by Lauro early in the 1900s for a private villa near Turin. This acquisition remains a solid example of the "Liberty style" or Stile Floreale – literally, floral style – which has come to exemplify the Italian design initiative of the period. Captivated by the great beauty and rarity of the complete room interior produced under the singular direction of Lauro, Mr. Wolfson now features the double parlor in his extensive collection of decorative art. Yet even the most perceptively chosen acquisition can cause problems. As our admiration of the parlor grew, our frustration over learning little about Agostino Lauro increased. Was he an architect, a designer (illus. 4), an entrepreneur – or all three? What influence did he exert at the Turin exposition of 1902? Why is so little known about Lauro today?

In his text, Dr. Gabriel P. Weisberg, Professor of Art History at the University of Minnesota in Minneapolis, answers many of these perplexing questions about Lauro and his contemporaries. He also outlines the evolution of early twentieth-century Italian interior design and the catalytic nature of the Turin exhibition in its promotion. Rather than being daunted by the paucity of material on Italian contributions to the Turin exposition, Dr. Weisberg plunged into the subject to ascertain the substantial achievements of designers working in the Stile Floreale, an area of art history largely ignored by scholars outside of Italy. To this intriguing examination of the Stile Floreale he brings a well-established sense of scholarly sleuthing and rediscovery. While his early findings provided the project with a level of excitement, exasperation and frustration soon set in. Where does one look for information when the exhibition's participants are no longer alive and many accounts of the Turin exposition are lost?

Renata Rutledge then joined the project team to unearth and translate Italian documents of the time. Her knowledge of and enthusiasm for the period quickly made her a vital asset to our endeavor, especially when she agreed to undertake a spontaneous trip to Turin to interview those familiar with the enigmatic Signor Lauro. Some of Dr. Weisberg's research utilizes factual data Mrs. Rutledge gathered from civil records, archival materials, and conversations with Lauro descendants in Italy.

Those who assisted her in this painstaking stitching together of information include many citizens and the administration of Turin. The Wolfsonian Foundation is grateful to those who generously joined in our search. Special thanks go to Dottoressa Rossana Bossaglia, whose extensive knowledge of Stile Floreale, evident in the preface to the catalogue, was of great value in the preparation of this exhibition. Others who deserve recognition are: author Maria Paola Maino; architect Giorgio Rigotti and Professor Roberto Gabetti, head of the architectural school in Turin; Mario Matta, president of the Assosazione Minusieri; Dottoressa Roccia, conservator at the Archivio Storico della Citta; Dottoressa Rosanna Maggio Serra and Cecilia Giudici Servetti of the Biblioteca Musei Civici of Turin;

AGOSTINO LAURO

TAPPEZZIERE
DI
S. A. R.
IL PRINCIPE DI CARIGNANO

TORINO

Via S. Teresa 21

Torino Litog. Luigi Giani

Dottoressa Renata Monti of the Biblioteca Civica; Alberta Zanella of the Biblioteca Centrale; Dottoressa Gemma Cambursano, Direttrice, Sopraintendenza dei beni ambientali ed architectonici del Piemonte; Contessa Malilli Balbo di Vinadio and Signora Paola Cometti; Fulvio Ferrari; Geom. P. Sburlati of the Scuola S. Carlo; Ing. Agostino Giannetto; Giuseppe Testa; Anna Maria and Vittorio Valabrega; Angelo Dragone of the newspaper *La Stampa*; Marina Trombetto; Maria Tallia; Gregory Wagenseil; Barry Friedman; and Yvonne Fuortes. Last but not least is Rosetta Ajmone-Marsan, who lives in Miami but offered considerable assistance to our efforts in Italy. We are also grateful to the staff of the Novecento Corporation and the Wolfsonian Foundation in Genoa, particularly Baron Paolo von Wedel and Dr. Matteo Fochessati.

Stile Floreale: The Cult of Nature in Italian Design and its accompanying catalogue represent a significant departure from the earlier theme presentations mounted at Miami-Dade Community College that primarily used works from the Wolfson Collection. In fact, Miami-Dade Community College and the Mitchell Wolfson Jr. Collection of Decorative and Propaganda Arts share an exhibition history that dates from *Brave New Worlds: America's Futurist Vision*, which opened at the College in January of 1984. This relationship came about through the foresight, sensitivity, and cooperative spirits of College president Robert H. McCabe and Mitchell Wolfson, Jr. The continuing support of the College District Board of Trustees – Chairman Daniel K. Gill, Vice-Chairman Garth C. Reeves, Sr., Ofelia Tabares Fernandez, Arva Moore Parks, Walter L. Revell, and Dr. José Antonio Alvarado – as well as that of Dr. Eduardo J. Padron, Wolfson Campus Vice-President and C.E.O., and Renée Betancourt, Dean for Development, has been crucial to the program.

Numerous colleagues in Miami assisted with the various organizational and planning aspects of this exhibition. On behalf of the Wolfsonian Foundation, I would like to thank Head Registrar Christine Giles and her able staff, Dennis Wilhelm and Carol Alper, who oversaw the complex details of shipping and handling objects and supervised the exhibition's installation. Carol also tracked down detailed information on the objects needed for the catalogue. Edgardo Bugin's skills in conservation are also worthy of praise. In addition, I want to thank Washington Storage Company for their special efforts. For their research and administrative assistance, I express my appreciation to Marge Newman and Lea Nickless of the Foundation staff. My thanks extend as well to my collegues at The Wolfson Initiative Corporation – Cathy Leff, Franz Capraro, and Hal Auerbach – for their support and encouragement.

At Miami-Dade Community College, Robert Sindelir, Director of Galleries and Visual Arts Programs, coordinated the many organizational tasks that befall the host institution and greatly assisted with this catalogue. The Wolfsonian Foundation is grateful to him and his staff, under whose guidance visitors will enjoy this landmark presentation.

I also thank George Sexton Associates for their inspired exhibition design and Moshe Goren for his clever and meticulous reconstruction of the Lauro double parlor. Jacques Auger Design Associates creatively handled the catalogue's design, and Nancy Eickel expertly edited its text.

Above all, I wish to thank Mitchell Wolfson, Jr., without whose singular vision and continuous support this unique collection and program would not exist. This exploration of Italian design and decorative arts marks the beginning of academic research into an area of art history too long slighted in the United States. Mr. Wolfson's knowledge of Italy and her cultural contributions will undoubtedly assure the Wolfsonian Foundation a place at the center of these scholarly pursuits.

As a serious examination of a major event in the history of art and design, *Stile Floreale: The Cult of Nature in Italian Design* focuses on the superb references found in the vast holdings of the Wolfson Collection. It features decorative objects and even an entire room installation, which most certainly will encourage scholars, students, and critics to conduct further research into Italy's awakening to the potential harmony of architectural and interior design and her own version of modern decorative art. At the same time, this exhibition signifies a new direction in the Wolfsonian Foundation's promotion of the decorative arts. When the Foundation's museum and study facility open in 1990, in-depth study of the social, artistic, historical, and political relationships that characterize the late nineteenth and twentieth centuries, particular areas of concentration for the Wolfson Collection, will be greatly facilitated.

Much remains to be learned about those whose activities earlier in this century initiated Italy's participation in an integrated design aesthetic. For now, I invite you to carry out your own exploration of *Stile Floreale: The Cult of Nature in Italian Design*.

Peggy A. Loar
Director
The Wolfsonian Foundation

INTERIOR DESIGN REFORM IN ITALY:
THE STILE FLOREALE
AND THE IMPLICATIONS OF THE
TURIN EXPOSITION, 1902

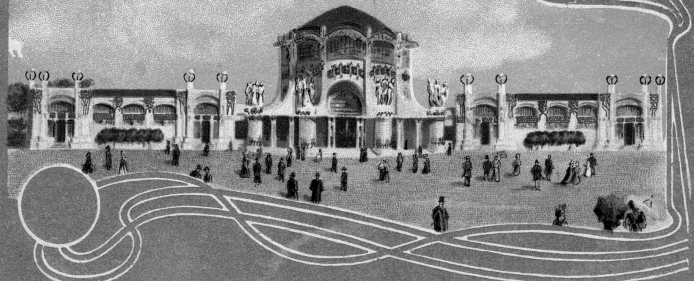

ESPOSIZIONE INTERNAZIONALE   D'ARTE DECORATIVA MODERNA

TORINO · 1902 ·

VESTIBOLO D'ONORE E FACCIATA PRINCIPALE

PART I: THE ROLE OF THE FIRST INTERNATIONAL EXPOSITION OF MODERN DECORATIVE ART, TURIN, 1902

In May of 1902, the opening of the *Prima Esposizione Internazionale d'Arte Decorativa Moderna* was a much heralded event. One writer outlined the significance of this international design exposition for his readers.

Today the Exposition – the first exposition in Italy free of academic and conventional shackles – is a fact, a living entity ... that deserves admiration. It is the first time that we in Italy have had the courage to break with tradition; ... it is beautiful and glorious when this happens in Italy.

It is the first time any of us has cut loose all the inferior artifice that imitates or regurgitates the elements of past styles, making a place instead for art that creates. Freed from having to satisfy clients, it puts itself in direct rapport with practical living and becomes the fountain of the applied arts.

The exhibition in Turin is international. Conditions cannot be the same for all nations. The movement tends to reconcile art and industry in this modern form that is required by new social relations and the diverse organization of modern life. It rapidly developed in Germany, England, Austria, and France, flourishing for more than ten years. In these countries, consumption has responded to production, and the best and richest forces in the field have been employed by industry. From this has emerged a rapid and beautiful flowering. Turin, too, offers flowers to admire that are no less beautiful and perfumed, although not the first or the freshest buds.

Initially, the opposite happened in Italy. There was little demand for a modern decorative art that could excite a stream of production. The few requests made and suggested by consumers who remembered things seen abroad could be easily satisfied with imported goods or some original work. Our artists, who should be excited by the competition of foreign movements and should emulate them, have instead been working in sterility for their own pleasure, or for ephemeral fame in an artistic clique, or for the glory solely of their province.

The exhibition in Turin ventures toward meeting the unknown, but with high ideals that are at the same time practical. It will produce immediate contact between foreign decorative arts and ours, an equalization that could permit our latent creative forces to compete in the future under equal conditions. ...

It is still early for us. We are less wealthy than the other countries, and our wealth is less cultivated, less refined. Moreover, the individualism by which everyone wants a home, furniture, or decor according to his taste and different from others is ... premature.

When Italy neither seeks inspiration from abroad nor works on commission or for publicity, we have misfortune, as Vittorio Pica, an authoritative critic, notes apropos certain endeavors by our artists.

Misfortunes?

There could be. But can decorative art really be modern if it does not take into account the economic factors of our time?[1]

2 Raimondo d'Aronco. Entrance to the
Pavilion of Interiors at the Turin exposi-
tion of 1902. From *L'Architettura alla
Prima Esposizione Internazionale d'Arte
Decorativa Moderna*, Turin, 1902.

3 Charles and Margaret Mackintosh.
Salottino delle Rose, at the Turin exposition of 1902. From Vittorio Pica, *L'Arte
Decorativa all'Esposizione di Torino del
1902*, Bergamo, 1903.

4 Victor Horta. *Salotto*, at the Turin exposition of 1902. From Vittorio Pica, *L'Arte
Decorativa all'Esposizione di Torino del
1902*, Bergamo, 1903.

1

The international exposition of decorative design that opened in Turin in the early summer of 1902 (figs. 1, 2) challenged outmoded preconceptions about Italian design as it helped dispel the notion that Italy remained an artistic backwater that could not compete with other countries in the production of modern interior design for the home. Through displays and impressive installations produced by leading craftsmen and entrepreneurs throughout Europe, the Turin exposition presented the day's newest design programs, especially those from Germany and Scotland, while it permitted Italian firms and designers the opportunity to showcase their accomplishments. Italian artists planned and carefully crafted room installations and individual pieces to prove that Italy had at last achieved the beginning of a new style. Since then, some critics and historians have dubbed this manner the "Liberty style" or the "Stile Floreale," considering it another aspect of the international art nouveau movement that spread over the European continent from 1895 until about 1904 or 1905.[2]

Instead of seeing the Turin exposition of modern decorative art as a final flowering of the crafts renaissance that dominated much of the nineteenth century, it is imperative to recognize it as a catalyst for the continued reformation of the decorative arts in Italy. In essence, it became a forum where Italian designers could compete internationally. Similarly, the Turin exposition planted the seeds of the progressive art deco style of the next decades. Even at this early date, the geometric abstractions offered by Scottish, Belgian, and German designers (figs. 3, 4) suggested that a new style was in the offing, one that would rely less on the nature-oriented qualities of art nouveau.

Since the 1902 Turin exposition has not been adequately studied – some historians consider it a total debacle – the names of many leading furniture and ensemble designers, in particular those of the Italian section, have lapsed into obscurity. It is essential, therefore, that the cultural context surrounding the emergence of the Stile Floreale be partially reconstructed to place the contributions of individual creators in perspective. This will facilitate assessing the achievements of some of the more prominent Italian designers who participated in this early international exhibition of decorative design. Several specific pieces of furniture have been located, and an effort has been made to reconstruct room interiors that might have been influenced by the Turin exposition of 1902 (and possibly presented at the exhibition itself). In this way, the veil of mystery that encircles the Stile Floreale can begin to be removed.

THE AESTHETIC CLIMATE IN ITALY AND ELSEWHERE PRIOR TO 1902

Italian decorative design before 1902 did not advance as quickly as elsewhere on the European continent, even though some firms and independent designers

were well aware of the progress made in England, France, and Germany. There, the design reform movement was sponsored in part by wealthy industrialists and enlightened supporters eager to revitalize the modern home. Avant-garde designers in England and France created environments that abandoned traditional, historical styles. Architects and interior designers remodeled spaces, allowing realistic or abstracted motifs derived from nature to flourish in rooms filled with a fresh sense of light, air, and space. The most successful designers innovatively utilized colors, stressed visual integration, and created harmonizing furniture and related objects.

Before 1902, a series of significant exhibitions had been organized to promote an exchange of ideas among designers from several countries, despite the fact that architects and artisans from Belgium and Germany ranked as the undisputed leaders of the design reform movement by the end of the 1890s. Among the most progressive of these international exhibitions were those held in Dresden (1897), where Belgian designer Henry van de Velde presented a series of provocative room interiors, and in Darmstadt (1901). For the latter, members of the Darmstadt art colony worked together to produce new forms and buildings that became paradigms for artistic inspiration and influence. At these and other exhibitions, Belgian and German designers challenged traditional modes and conventions by making it amply clear that their adherence to classical conventions and revival styles was over.

The Dresden exhibition (another one that has received scant historical attention due to the paucity of surviving documents and installation ensembles) was especially successful in the areas of furniture design and modern room ensembles created for private patrons.[3] In this exhibition, room interiors by van de Velde provoked heated discussions. Originally shown at Siegfried Bing's first salon of art nouveau in Paris in December of 1895, these rooms certified that integrated interior decoration was the wave of the future.[4] Judging from press reports of the time, attendance at the exhibition was quite high, and these newly designed interior spaces significantly influenced decorators and architects in cities throughout Europe, including Paris and eventually Turin.

At the same time these design competitions were being held, businessmen, acutely aware of the need to produce designs that would attract the "new wealth" in the cities, developed marketing strategies that would entice such an audience. Bing in Paris, along with his cohort and sympathetic colleague, the art dealer Julius Meier-Graefe, responded to these initiatives by opening their galleries to international currents (figs. 5, 6). They strongly believed that designers should be directly supported by active entrepreneurs with the financial means to bolster their ideas and the artistic taste to promote decorative styles. Both Bing's gallery, *L'Art Nouveau,* and later Meier-Graefe's showroom, *La Maison Moderne,* became models for what could be accomplished if designers and businessmen worked toward the common goal of invigorating living spaces.

SALLE PRINCIPALE DE "LA MAISON MODERNE" A L'EXPOSITION DE TURIN.1902.

Similarly, the firm of Liberty and Company in London, intending to enlarge the international scope of its efforts, marketed fabrics and other objects that could be used in conjunction with furniture and woodworking. Liberty and Company supplied Italian decorators with actual Liberty fabrics for the walls of their home environments. It also persuaded other Italian firms to create patterns based on Liberty motifs and samples.[5] As decorators increasingly used Liberty-inspired fabrics on their furniture and walls, the relationship grew. This link and the potential for extensive ties with the Liberty firm caused some of the earliest initiatives in Italian design reform to be called the "Liberty style." In time, this label reinforced the growing sense of independence and freedom in Italian design as well as established ties with the English arts and crafts movement.[6]

By the close of the 1890s, Italy began to organize its own design competitions. One held in Turin in 1898 pointed towards the directions some designers were headed. Although artisans who were still heavily indebted to historical styles predominated, this exhibition did provide other decorators and firms with an opportunity to illustrate how they were attempting to utilize models derived from foreign countries. Among these designers was Agostino Lauro, a furniture manufacturer in Turin.

Lauro was destined to become a major player at the Turin exposition of 1902 through the construction of his own *palazzina*. This building, similar to the Austrian and German entries, used teams of artisans from all design fields to create a unified, decorative scheme for a series of room interiors. Although the completed interiors were sharply criticized by the press, Lauro's entrepreneurial skill (like that of Bing and Meier-Graefe in Paris) substantiated that here was an able coordinator who could produce under severe time constraints. As a businessman and a manufacturer, Lauro (fig. 7) learned many lessons from his European counterparts. He willingly directed his services and business skills towards the higher ideals of art, believing that his designer/decorator teams could manufacture environments that would rival any international creation.

Yet it was the 1900 Exposition Universelle in Paris, more than individual efforts or smaller European exhibitions, that illustrated both the international range of the design reform movement and Italy's creative failings. At this fair, modern achievements in France, Great Britain, and certain Scandinavian countries became harbingers of a new style. The pavilion *Art Nouveau Bing* (fig. 8) attracted worldwide acclaim; the architecture of other sections implied that a concerted design movement had begun, one that exerted pressure on the ways modern interiors were created in Austria, Germany, Scotland, and England. Italy's tentative strivings could not fully compete at this time with the progress attained by designers from other countries.[7] In essence, the Paris fair of 1900 emphasized that Italy must rapidly move forward in design or remain hopelessly locked in outmoded traditions.

Plans were then launched for Italy to host an international design exhibition in Turin, where there was considerable monetary support for such an endeavor. Through its impressive magnitude, this exhibition would show the best of Italian design in tandem with the achievements of other European nations. Many believed that Turin was an appropriate city for this exposition, because it lacked a long tradition in the decorative arts and was therefore less ``enslaved'' by historicisms. Designers and manufacturers would also find a freer atmosphere in which to present model rooms, for they would be welcomed more readily in Turin than in the more deeply entrenched, conservative circles of other cities.

Clearly, the exhibition's sponsors hoped that a full reflowering of Italian genius in a seriously neglected field would continue after the exposition. Presenting models and innovations from other countries, they surmised, would generate debate among Italian designers and provoke them into action. To a limited degree, this process had been successful in Belgium and France, and critics and manufacturers who would attend the Turin exposition envisioned similar results.

By 1900, the wave of design competition formulated in the previous decade came to a climax. Its final flowering, the epitome of the Stile Floreale, did indeed occur at the Turin exposition of 1902. There, Italian furniture and room ensembles revealed both a sensitivity to design innovations and a commitment to the full utilization of natural details and organic qualities.

THE TURIN EXPOSITION OF 1902: A PROGRAM INTO PRACTICE

Drawing on leaders in the design reform movement throughout the world, the Turin exposition convened a ``jury'' of international figures, who set a prestigious tone for the exhibition and all related conferences. Among the jury members were Walter Crane, the exposition's Honorary President who represented the enlightened tendencies of the arts and crafts tradition in England, and Albert Besnard, a romantic portrait painter and a powerful artistic politician in France when the Paris Salon was reformed and the Société Nationale des Beaux-Arts was organized as a counter group in the 1890s.[8] E. de Radisics from Hungary, H. Fierens-Gevaert, a symbolist painter from Belgium, and Giovanni Teserone and David Calandra from Italy rounded out the distinguished panel.[9]

Other members of the jury, culled from participating countries, set parameters for the exhibition and awarded prizes to the individuals or firms whose work was judged to be of the highest quality. Since the jury did not want any one designer to dominate, awards were presented strictly to countries, with the opportunity for the native designers to draft the wording of the award certificate. In this way, no nation appeared superior, and each country could adequately recognize its artists whose contributions best exemplified achievements in design reform.

8 Photographer unknown. Photograph of the pavilion *Art Nouveau Bing* at the Exposition Universelle, Paris, 1900. Courtesy: G.P. Weisberg.

Elements essential to a renaissance in the decorative arts formed the guiding principles of the exposition, as noted in the jury's program and interpreted by critics in the daily press. Jury members sought to promote the impression of "life" in the exhibited works and voiced strong antipathy towards eclectic, historical styles that were largely influenced by the classical past.[10] They encouraged the so-called minor arts to maintain their equality and visibility. Decorative designers were urged to resist the creative suffocation of commercial magnates who bastardized objects for mass production. The organizers of the Turin exposition refused to allow the progress of the past decade to be impeded. Instead, Italian design reform was nurtured through a massive display of international talent, which influenced the careers of many younger designers.

In explaining the exposition, the prominent critic Enrico Thovez presented other criteria.

> We want this (exposition) of ours to have a completely new character, thereby providing our visitors not with a spectacle of various purposes and styles, but a series of decorative complexes, complete ambiences (that) respond to the true needs of our existence. We would like this fundamental show of decor not only to aim at an aristocratic style of elegance and beautiful arts but also to a practical and industrial style. We would like ... artists and manufacturers not to tend too much towards precious objects of luxury, but rather (towards) coordinated decoration adaptable to all kinds of houses and all means, especially for those of lower income, so as to bring about a real, efficacious, and complete renovation of the environment.[11]

This emphasis on complete room interiors grew from trends seen in other countries. The desire to have them fully integrated was deeply ingrained in the guidelines established by the Turin jury and exposition committee. Thovez went on to stress that artists and manufacturers should

> explore complete installations, harmoniously constituted. This is preferred over single objects for reasons of clarity, with the suggestion that we follow this invitation with a detailed program for various branches. ...[12]

Aesthetics were certainly important. To achieve the appearance of visual accord, critics expected designers to follow two standards: simplicity of form and logic. Thovez seized on these qualities, which were undoubtedly a primary topic at the exposition.

> Beauty for the most part should emerge through the intelligent adaptation of material to its use. One must be warned, moreover, to struggle commercially against actual production. ... It is required to seek economically the material and simplicity of workmanship, a compensation for the high cost of introducing new models in industry. ... It is time to demonstrate through examples that beauty need not be the result only of rich materials with a profusion of ornamentation, but rather of elegance, harmony of color, and perfection of execution.[13]

These issues preoccupied those who served as jurors at Turin. As the awards were distributed to members of the different delegations, those recognized were

generally the artists/craftsmen who had already made outstanding contributions to specific areas of decorative design in their homelands. This certainly held true with the French participants. Alexandre Bigot, a leading ceramist, received a diploma of honor for his years of service to the field as well as for his dominant position as a technically proficient designer who applied modern aesthetics to ceramic decorations for the home.[14] Popular journals, such as the magazine *Art et Décoration,* were given awards for fostering awareness of design reform. Individual craftsmen in glass, in particular the Daum firm, and jewelry (Eugène Feuillâtre) received silver medals for their innovations.

Significantly, Siegfried Bing, a respected tastemaker and entrepreneur, unanimously received a diploma of merit for his efforts to popularize a decorative style for modern interiors.[15] Bing's prestige, his accomplishments at the Paris Exposition Universelle of 1900, and his continuing ability to promote total room environments, reinforced the central role of French designers, and especially of independent businessmen, in revitalizing decorative design. Such acknowledgment of Bing's pioneering efforts in the design reform movement also augmented the sense of equity and historical accuracy that permeated the Turin exposition.[16]

A similar enlightened attitude prevailed in the awards presented to Belgian designers. Victor Horta, an original Belgian architect, received deserved attention for his contributions to modern home construction. Philippe Wolfers, a goldsmith, was awarded a diploma of honor. Gold medals were presented to the symbolist painter Ferdinand Khnopff and to the sculptor Fernand Dubois to illustrate further the esteem in which these artists were held. Curiously, the Belgian section chose not to recognize the adventurous designs of Henry van de Velde (fig. 9), perhaps in part because he was increasingly linked with Germany.[17]

In the American section several awards were given to the founding promoters of design reform in the United States: Tiffany and Company of New York, Paul Wayland Bartlett, a symbolist sculptor who had worked actively in France during the 1890s, and the Rookwood Pottery Company of Cincinnati, Ohio.[18] These designers had challenged European preeminence for years, so their awards were not startling. Once again, however, the written justification for these medals demonstrated insight into the fundamental achievements of these groups. All three were praised by their artistic peers for their creativity within an enlightened system of patronage.[19] Other American manufacturers were presented awards for artistic objects. Both the Gorham Manufacturing Company of New York and the Grueby Faience Company of Boston received a gold medal. Since America was viewed as a pioneer in combining art with industry, these firms symbolized for many what could be accomplished when manufacturers maintained control over creative originality and did not allow commercial gain to become the sole reason for existence. They also served as archetypes for what Italian manufacturers were then trying to accomplish.

10 Peter Behrens. *Gabinetto di Lavoro per l'Editore A. Koch,* at the Turin exposition of 1902. From Vittorio Pica, *L'Arte Decorativa all'Esposizione di Torino del 1902,* Bergamo, 1903.

PETER BEHRENS: GABINETTO DI LAVORO PER L'EDITORE A. KOCH.

JOSEF OLBRICH: STANZA DA PRANZO.

Aesthetic achievements of other artistic firms were duly noted as well. The major Danish award went to the Royal Copenhagen Manufactory of Porcelain, which had produced imaginative pieces with natural and Japanese-inspired motifs since the 1880s. Silver medals were presented to the innovative porcelain manufactory of Bing and Grondhal in Copenhagen and to a firm that had extensively shown in Europe at such emporiums as Meier-Graefe's *La Maison Moderne* in Paris.[20] Yet the countries most eagerly examined at Turin were those whose inventive creators embodied the goals of the exposition, namely, the contributions of Scotland and Germany.

Jurors at the Turin exposition were obviously aware of how material, space, and color tones could be agreeably arranged to reinforce and promote the concept of sensitively modulated interior spaces. In the furniture and room interiors by Charles Rennie Mackintosh and Margaret MacDonald, they correctly identified the future direction of design reform. These designers from Glasgow received a diploma of honor for their harmoniously integrated and logically conceived furniture (fig. 3). Through their "complete installations" for the modern home, Mackintosh and MacDonald were considered the most proficient designers exhibiting at Turin.

The German section was likewise praised and studied. Rightfully, the jurors were impressed with the Germans' entry of thirty-five to forty room installations, which included a room by the architect Peter Behrens (fig. 10) and one by Josef

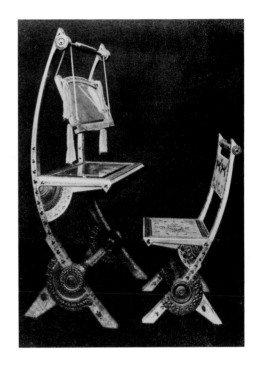

Olbrich (fig. 11). A large reception hall and a library Behrens designed for the Darmstadt art colony were featured as well. The effectiveness of the Darmstadt revolution in aesthetics and the complexity of their subtle reordering of interiors and space were obvious to perceptive visitors. These rooms appropriately gauged how far interior design had progressed in Germany.

Such works clarified that Italian designers faced rigorous standards. Questions of technique, visual unity, originality, and overall design were just a few of the issues debated in the native press. Italian critics, like those in France and England, compared Italian designers with their foreign counterparts. They identified areas of improvement, detected recent signs of progress, and determined whether a recognizable style appropriate to Italy appeared in the objects and room installations shown at Turin. Debates were intense. Some extremely hostile reviews criticized individual designers and pieces, claiming that the Turin exposition posed a series of festering questions about design reform. An analysis of press reviews will determine how far Italian design had advanced, how it was perceived on native soil, and to what extent the importation of outside models served as creative and educational agitators.

THE ITALIAN SECTION OF THE TURIN EXPOSITION AND THE PRESS

When the Turin exposition opened in 1902, the international and native press apparently perceived Italian decorative design as weak. Some critics correctly surmised that an international decorative arts exhibition was being held in Turin to spur Italian artistic creativity through direct confrontation with external models. Since this technique had worked in other countries, notably in Belgium, France, Germany, and Scandinavia, comparable results were anticipated in Italy. In addition, Italian manufacturers would hopefully exert themselves competitively, so their designs could catch up with and eventually challenge European advances.

To promote a forceful public debate, the Italian press was primed to assess works by both foreigners and natives. Unfortunately, from the Italian perspective, debates often became strident. Critics, who could not always identify the fundamental issues at hand, often antagonized the designers instead.

Examination of the Italian section produced a divided critical assessment. Some thoughtful reviews reflected a long familiarity with international design. Others, primarily native in outlook, projected naive and provincial viewpoints. The former were most effective in casting the Italian achievements against a larger background. The latter, with their belligerent tone, often failed to provide the kind of criticism that could assist fledgling Italian designers to view their works in a broader context.

Georg Fuchs, one of the more enlightened young writers from Germany, felt that Italian design efforts reflected a melange of attitudes and forms. Too many of the Italian pieces, he maintained, looked like a "bazaar" or a "carnival" where

13 Carlo Bugatti. Library steps or stool. Walnut, pewter, vellum, and copper, Italy, ca. 1902. Courtesy: Mitchell Wolfson Jr. Collection. Cat. no. 26.

everything was attempted. He remarked that designers adopted motifs too freely and failed to establish their own sense of personal style and vision. "Everything that was ever invented in modern stylistic fantasy in Europe is here in evidence and moreover, it is all gaudily exaggerated and overdecorated."[21]

Fuchs was also deeply concerned that design simplicity and the logic of an architectural underpinning were not completely understood. At the same time, however, he admitted that the Italians displayed an amazing "technical ability" with great potential. "What would happen," he wrote, "if this other Italy ... were to take over with a strong hand to control this chaos?"[22] This tantalizing comment most certainly would not have escaped designers and critics. Yet the German writer found only a few models that Italians could follow. He lauded Carlo Bugatti as original and inventive (fig. 12) and the one individual who could lead Italy out of "darkness and confusion." In his remarks, Fuchs felt Bugatti's work displayed an awareness of materials, often combined with a sense of playfulness and whimsy (fig. 13), that went far beyond the creations of other Italian designers. Fuchs was clearly Bugatti's primary champion.

In general, the German critic noted that skillful pastiches dominated the Italian section (figs. 14, 15), and he downplayed the continuing reliance on grand, traditional production. Again he asserted that the Italians imitated models drawn from "mediocre English, German, and French samples." He reiterated that Italy had to change its practices to be competitive. It simply had to stop borrowing and "learn to work on its own." For a new style to emerge fully in Italy, creative designers must be freed from restrictions, but Fuchs could find few individuals with such an essential and timely vision. Still, if a "new designer" could be discovered in Italy, Fuchs believed it would be possible for Italian designers to produce room interiors of exceptional quality. Numerous industrial firms that manufactured sample rooms demonstrated a high technical skill which could be meshed with creative originality. On this topic, Fuchs mentioned the achievements of Vittorio Valabrega and Agostino Lauro, two firms that impressed him at Turin.

Although persuasive on many counts, Fuchs' critique was colored by his own background. He simply could not see any creative inclinations beyond the apparent ones. Even if Fuchs was generally correct in his assessments, especially when he accused Italy of failing to produce truly creative designs, he also was fallible.

Many of Fuchs' international colleagues shared his contention that the Italian section was wanting. Others either commented briefly on what the Italians had attempted or simply chose to ignore it. A few critics controlled their caustic tones towards Italian design, perhaps because they were guests in Turin, although several of them did refer to Fuchs' general observations in their own reviews. The prominent designer Walter Crane gave his "general impressions" of the Turin exposition in a leading British journal.[23] Sensing the exhibition's critical

14 Raimondo d'Aronco. Interior of the Central Salon of the Italian Gallery at the Turin exposition of 1902. From *L'Architettura alla Prima Esposizione Internazionale d'Arte Decorativa Moderna*, Turin, 1902.

nature, Crane wrote that the Italians had achieved ``brilliant, dramatic'' and even ``extraordinary technical skill in all materials'' by creating the impression of a tour de force that ``often arrested attention.'' These broad statements, however, did not camouflage Crane's astute awareness that Italian design was ``careless of observing the limits of balanced expression.''[24] Crane could scarcely overlook such exaggerated tendencies. He reiterated the call for simplicity and logic that had guided the jury's recommendations.

Such cautionary statements were less problematic than the remarks made by a number of native critics. These writers, who continued to provoke heated, open debates, were sometimes quite unkind towards the achievements of a nascent ``new style'' in Italy.

Some commentators on the effects of the Turin exposition were quick to
note that Italian critics not only were ill informed about international
developments but also were likely to condemn design advances due to their own
poor training. Enrico Thovez, an insightful critic, wrote, "Let us speak plainly: . . .
the Italian critics were not able to recognize the importance of the Exposition.
One can prove that time and again they were unjustly indifferent, inexact, hasty,
and contemptuous. The key is that they were (aside from a few) ill prepared. . . ."[25]
Not enough writers, Thovez recognized, were able to provide valuable comments
or deeper insights into what the Italians hoped to accomplish.

Other critics, including Romualdo Pantini, tried to explain why Turin had
been selected as the location for an international design exhibition. He placed
the site in historical context by expounding on the significance of the city's
architecture, the value of the national applied arts exhibitions that had already

been held there, and the community's ability to foster new ideas, especially ones in design reform that affected architecture and all the applied arts. Pantini added, "This Turin exposition carries in itself the inspiring, excellent principle that the evolution of life is necessary to the evolution of form."[26] This contextualization in contemporary literature was extremely important. It helped readers to understand what was occurring as it countered some of the more negative notices in the press. Also, Turin's central role in the visual arts, in particular, was a significant point that international critics often missed completely.

A second critic, Efisto Aitelli, also expressed sensitivity to the aims and achievements of the exposition. Since Aitelli realized that the Italian tradition of art education was weak, if not thoroughly conservative, he quickly emphasized that "the exposition has achieved a noble aim. It shows that the activities of those who work seriously and diligently can succeed.... We now have renounced the past and follow the spirit of modernity, but all our efforts are diffused ... we need stronger educational foundations."[27]

Aitelli accurately drew attention to the deficiency of applied arts education in Italy, a concern shared in other European countries. Even more perceptive was his call for a revival of individualism and the fostering of originality. He argued against graduating students who could think only according to prescribed formulas. As one of the exposition's more observant critics, Aitelli identified some of the better Italian designers. Yet unlike other writers, he refused to denigrate everything Italian and chose to remain positive in tone.

Of all the commentators on the Turin exposition who took time to examine closely specific pieces in the Italian section, the most persuasive and informed was Vittorio Pica. By publishing his book in 1903, Pica could assess the entire exposition and place Italian contributions in perspective.

In *L'Arte Decorativa all'Esposizione di Torino del 1902*, Pica provided a historical background of the Turin exposition. He carefully noted that the Italians had been extremely slow to react to the pressures of modern design reform, citing that only rarely before 1900 could contributions of real value be identified. When the strivings toward a new style did occur, Pica observed that designers were eager to study nature with a fresh eye, to develop motifs from plants and flowers, and to move away from the confines of the classic.[28] Pica evidently believed that the design exhibition held in Turin in 1898 had provided a sufficient liberating stimulus from past styles.

Yet when it came to assessing Italian contributions to the 1902 Turin exposition, Pica revealed both a sense of caution and an intimate familiarity with specific works, firms, and individual creators. In many cases, Pica focused on the best furniture designers in the Italian section. Here, he found the jury too lenient, generally for admitting all types of pieces. Nevertheless, he praised the work of Carlo Bugatti for "its conspicuous originality" (fig. 13), the achievements of Eugenio Quarti, who represented "a modern concept in accordance with the

17 Vittorio Ducrot, *Camera da Letto*, at the Turin exposition of 1902. From Vittorio Pica, *L'Arte Decorativa all'Esposizione di Torino del 1902*, Bergamo, 1903.

16 Eugenio Quarti. *Armadio per Salotto*, at the Turin exposition of 1902. From Vittorio Pica, *L'Arte Decorativa all'Esposizione di Torino del 1902*, Bergamo, 1903.

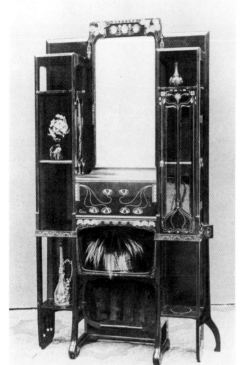

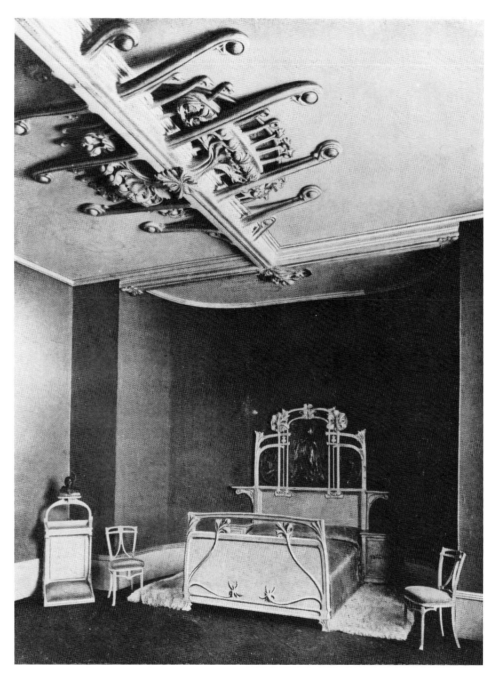

18 Agostino Lauro. Palazzina Lauro, at the
Turin exposition of 1902. From
*L'Architettura alla Prima Esposizione
Internazionale d'Arte Decorativa
Moderna,* Turin, 1902.

aesthetics of his people'' (fig. 16), and the innovative spirit of Carlo Zen's firm in
Milan. Pica, ever sensitive to the handling of materials and to the creation of new
designs that did not imitate those from other European centers, also admired the
work of Ernesto Basile and Vittorio Ducrot (fig. 17). He acknowledged that ''each
one of the three rooms presented by Basile and Ducrot is pleasing for some
special quality. . . . Obviously they are manufactured to serve with the greatest
practicality.''[29]

The thoughtful writer placed considerable attention on the furniture and
room ensembles at Turin, since he claimed that only by studying these examples
could the ''impact of art on the daily life'' of the people or the nation be judged.

He compared Italian designers to the French and the Scottish to determine whether they created room interiors of merit. Contrary to many other writers, he sympathetically evaluated several entries and detected in them the beginnings of an original style, the initial stages of the Stile Floreale.

Although not clearly visible in every Italian example, traces of this new style were indeed evident. Many critics missed them. Perhaps they moved through the Italian section too quickly, or their national biases blinded them to the aesthetic value of Italian designs based on nature studies. Pica later added that he rejected the "epithet of motley patchwork" that the German critic Fuchs had leveled against the applied arts of Italy.[30] He did note, nonetheless, that Italian design had not reached a degree of "necessary maturity." Since it was still influenced by foreigners, Pica could not fully announce that "there is already a new decorative Italian art, as it undoubtedly exists in England, Belgium, and Austria."[31] Despite his cautious assessments, his discriminating eye did distinguish evolving currents in Italian applied design.

As the debate over decorative reform widened, it encompassed not only isolated objects but also entire buildings created in Italian applied art design. The accuracy of Pica's appraisal became increasingly evident to those who examined one of the most elaborate and complicated contributions to Italian design at the Turin exposition, namely, the innovative pavilion created by Agostino Lauro (figs. 18-20). This *palazzina,* which employed the talents of numerous artisans/craftsmen, served as Italy's answer to the independent entrepreneur as tastemaker.

21 Rear view of the Austrian pavilion at the
Turin exposition of 1902. From
*L'Architettura alla Prima Esposizione
Internazionale d'Arte Decorativa
Moderna,* Turin, 1902.

2

Critical to the outcome of the Turin exposition was the commonly held belief that advances in Italian design, particularly those in the private sector, had to compare favorably with those of other countries. French achievements at the Paris Exposition Universelle of 1900 indicated to Italian design leaders that private entrepreneurs, working with select groups of artisans/craftsmen, could prove that art and industry had indeed come of age in Italy. The production of single, unique pieces and delicate room environments had already shown that such collaborative effort was possible. Potentially even more effective for winning the international design battle, they concluded, would be the creation of an entire villa – a palazzina – with a comprehensive architectural design, visually unified room interiors, and totally integrated furniture. If done creatively, this villa could establish that an unparalled Italian style for the modern home was available to those with avant-garde taste and sufficient money.

In Turin, Agostino Lauro, the owner of a well-known furniture manufacturing firm, strove to be the designer/entrepreneur whose palazzina would be the exposition's focus of controversy and measure of achievement. Lauro was soon considered a dynamic, perceptive leader thoroughly dedicated to harmonious design ensembles. His productions, the work of a wide range of skilled craftsmen, placed his firm at the vanguard of the design confrontations waged at the Turin exposition.

Lauro, who probably traveled to Paris in 1900, must have been aware of Siegfried Bing's innovations and his pavilion of art nouveau, a highlight of the Exposition Universelle. If not, some of Bing's favorably received room interiors from 1900 were shown again at Turin two years later. While the Turin decorator certainly respected Bing's achievements as a forerunner of interior decoration, he must also have realized that Bing's model rooms epitomized the Paris style of 1900. In addition, they underscored one of the basic arguments of the European design debate: the critical importance of creating total room interiors to reflect a modern style of home decoration. Thus, Bing's triumph in 1900 became in effect the standard for the independent, entrepreneurial approach. His ability to coordinate a corps of craftsmen, many of whom still remain anonymous, was generally regarded as crucial to enabling an entrepreneur to formulate his personal vision of the contemporary residential environment. Also, Bing's willingness to use his own capital symbolized the freedom and initiative an aesthetically educated entrepreneur might exercise. Unfortunately, few figures possessed Bing's dynamic leadership qualities, the financial acumen to back such an endeavor, and the political and artistic connections to make everything happen. Others were definitely eager to follow Bing's lead, but few could compare with such verve and ingenuity.

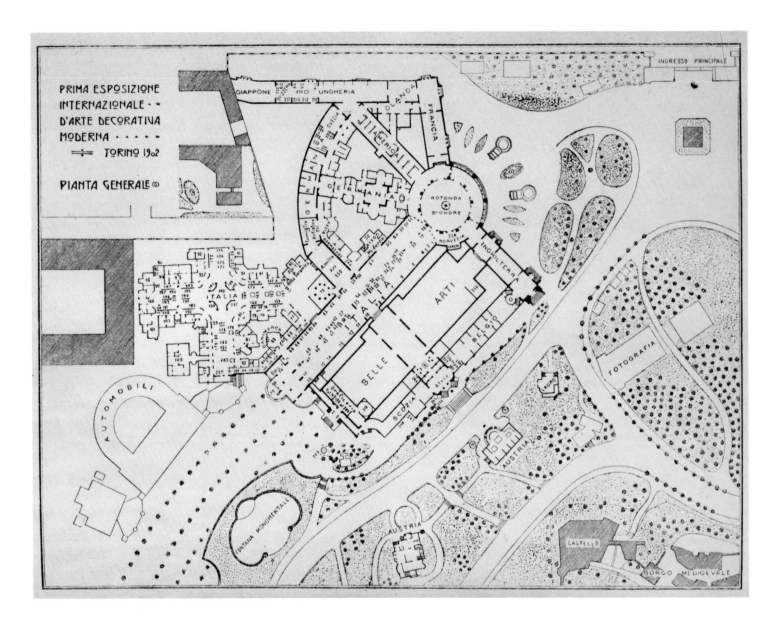

Despite this, Lauro wanted to initiate a similar enterprise at the Turin exposition. Although little is known of Lauro's organizational structure or his independent wealth, the construction of his own palazzina near the Austrian pavilion (fig. 21) was obviously a major endeavor. He had to obtain from the exposition's leaders considerable political support for such an undertaking, since the project implied a symbolic, yet essential gesture on their part that Italians, too, could devise a ``modern style.'' The construction and decoration of the palazzina, from the layouts of rooms to the handling of staircases and the manufacturing of furniture, had to be coordinated with skill and precision. Exposition organizers would not have entrusted Lauro with such a complex task if he had not been well respected in the artists' circles in Turin and throughout Italy.

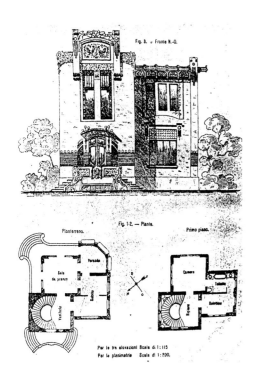

23 Front elevation and floor plan of the Palazzina Lauro, Turin, 1902. Private collection.

Lauro's completed palazzina, which received a gold medal, was not without its detractors. The story of the palazzina provides further insight into the design achievements at Turin and the roles played by independent businessmen.

THE AWARDING OF THE GOLD MEDAL: THE ITALIAN SECTION

Aside from works exhibited by Scottish and German designers, perhaps no other section provoked as much controversy and study as the Italian pavilion, which was designed by the renowned architect Raimondo d'Aronco. Italy's poor presentation at the Paris Exposition Universelle of 1900 had incited considerable consternation among knowledgeable collectors and critics. Ranked last among the Western nations committed to design reform, Italy encountered many problems, including the reluctance of its designers to replace historical styles with the adventurous changes then emanating from other countries.[32] Undoubtedly, observers at Turin were surprised by the noticeable signs of improvement in Italian design and by the number of artists and craftsmen who responded to the call for change and modernization. A few critics modestly praised the qualities of "eagerness and assurance" now detected in certain pieces of furniture.[33] When the attention was deflected from individual pieces, most of it came to rest on the palazzina by Agostino Lauro.[34]

Located near the Austrian pavilion (fig. 22), the Palazzina Lauro promoted the total unification of design when applied to a modern building. Both the exterior and the interior were subjected to radical transformations in keeping with "the tastes of the day."[35] In this creation

> by one of Torino's best known decorators, who had already distinguished himself at the 1898 Exposition, Agostino Lauro managed to assemble the talents of numerous firms and industrialists for a collective show. This exhibition, which was awarded a gold medal, succeeded quite well from many points of view, although it did not escape criticism. It also opened exceedingly late ... and some of its exhibitors, after having waited for the last moment to put in their installations, produced the most strident and enormous discord.[36]

Designed by the young architect Giuseppe Velati-Bellini, the palazzina embodied asymmetry controlled by a rational ordering of space and color (fig. 23). The extremely tall and narrow stained glass windows allowed softly modulated light to penetrate the building's interior with a delicate warmth. Corners of the blocky structure and the central cornice high above the main entranceway emphasized the architect's use of floral vegetation to suggest a building populated with life. On the string courses at the base, Velati-Bellini and other decorators used variegated ceramic tiles. There, they applied motifs abstracted from nature, which resembled similar designs on buildings constructed in Austria and in interior designs created in Scotland.

In a sense, the palazzina displayed partial amalgamations of Austrian and German efforts as well as the influence of the artists colony in Darmstadt. All this

was combined with the evolving Italian predilection for the effusive Stile Floreale. According to one critic,

> the villa appears varied and animated, because of the fluidity of the floor plan and the variety of the elevations in the various parts. The section that contains the stairs is like a tower. ... The other wings, however, with a flat roof, are lower. ... They are provided with elegant projecting cornices, interrupted at the south and west corners by small, elevated pillars forming cantonals. This crowning entablature is made of wood with some gilding and ceramic panels, placed vertically on the frieze and horizontally on the projecting edge. ... The main entrance is topped by a canopy of yellow glass, provided with spherical lamps. The flight of access steps is furnished with an unusual parapet of stone from Verona that serves as a bench. ...[37]

Velati-Bellini eventually emerged as one of the leading architects to create middle-class homes in the Stile Floreale, and the palazzina became his stepping stone to commissions in Turin and elsewhere.

Beyond its striking exterior appearance, the building employed an eye-catching and modern color scheme, one similar to the evolving interest in brilliant tones found in numerous Italian ceramics exhibited in 1902. Greens appeared on the walls; the medallions, painted blue, were encircled with gold for accent. The bouquets of roses on the exterior and interior were given a neutral color. Effective decorative details were found around the windows, on the central pediment, and on the cornice. Here, the architect, in collaboration with local tile manufacturers, explored a modest design in a limited range of colors. One critic commented on this effect, noting that

> the ground floor windows have tympanums of tiles that alternate in two colors (green and white, blue and white) of simple design. The casement of the upstairs windows is all around and holds designs of flowers in natural colors climbing around reeds of cane. There are also gourds, grapes, wisteria, balsam, poppies, roses, chrysanthemums, and water lilies. Thistles and Indian chestnut decorate the little windows that illuminate the stairs. Brightly colored groups of fruit, such as lemons, grapes, figs, pine cones, etc., sparkle on the frieze of the moldings. On the caissons of the eaves, between brackets, are small arabesque tiles in a deep green on a lighter green background. Finally we have the panel on the pediment, representing two roosters surrounded by ears of corn and poppies. A novelty is a mosaic with iridescent qualities from the Casa Cantagalli (the manufacturer). At certain hours of the morning and evening this mosaic produces unusual rays of fire to the detriment of the architectural effect. ... This pediment, surmounting the entrance, is topped by ornamentations sculpted in iron.[39]

This description, the most complete so far located, conveys the building's coloristic impact. Such alternative color zones and the interaction of ceramic tiles and metalwork stayed within the exposition's requirements that all crafts work in unison. The presence of various types of flowers and fruits fulfilled another fundamental goal: the building became a showpiece of artistic decoration associated with the Stile Floreale. These stylistic tendencies also appeared throughout the modern room installations Lauro commissioned from a series of Italian designers.

Most critically, however, the palazzina's avowed purpose – to create a building that would not go unnoticed at the Turin exposition – was definitely exceeded. Yet despite its significance and the importance then placed on the varied room installations (figs. 24, 25), a complete photographic record of the palazzina has not been located. This lack of visual record severely restricts an accurate critical appraisal of Italian achievements in room interiors and furniture design. Statements by observers, especially those by the meticulous critic A. Frizzi, quoted below, remain the best descriptions.

> Let's briefly examine the interior since it is decorated with great luxury, if not always with appropriate good taste. In the vestibule one finds an elliptical ramp composing the staircase, which unfolds beautifully. ... The walls are light. The floral decorations on the ceiling are reiterated in the massive landing of the first floor. Some cornices in stucco have a gilded ground. ...
>
> Soft light pervades the Salon, which is divided into two parts by a wall of glass. The furniture is upholstered in nut brown. The ceiling has beams with little flowers and a filet of gold intertwined on a café-au-lait background, while a band of the same design runs along the top of the walls.
>
> The dining room is illuminated by two great portals in semicircles that open onto terraces leading to the garden. Their striped glass panes are painted with fruit. Other groups of fruit figure at four pinnacles on the circular ceiling. ... Noteworthy are the credenza, the substantial round table, and various decorations in hammered copper on the walls. ...
>
> On the lower floor we also find a small room or veranda with blue and white striped walls and a blue ceiling with yellow roses, creating a vulgar effect. The glass doors have a special ornamental framework achieved with wood curved under the impact of steam.
>
> Extremely original are the furnishings of the upper little sitting room, which one must content oneself to examine from the doorway. ... The ceiling has an ornamentation in toned colors, leaving a more or less white square in the center.
>
> Very gracious is the bedroom completed for a single person, a true nest for a little lady. The walls and furniture are covered with silk fabric scattered with roses. The ceiling is in white with delicate red ribbons with pale wisteria and narcissi. These are well executed and in harmony with the elegant decor of the room.[40]

Since Velati-Bellini envisioned this as a modern townhouse for the wealthy middle-class, each room was designed for a specific use by family members at different times of the day. Decorations not only mirrored the room's function but also melded with the personality of the supposed owner. An impression of imposed elegance, based on Scottish, Austrian, and French prototypes, was conveyed through applied design and the intricate relationship of all the rooms to the overall floor plan.

26 Agostino Lauro and others. Detail of a
room in the palazzina, Turin, 1902.

27 Agostino Lauro. Preliminary drawing for a
room section at Sordevolo, ca. 1900-01.
Courtesy: Mitchell Wolfson Jr. Collection.
Cat. no. 12.

As general supervisor of the project, Lauro promoted the creation of curved
wood furniture decorated with elaborate inlays. He also encouraged the
incorporation of motifs that were both popular and typical of the burgeoning,
creative application of materials (fig. 26). His commitment to rich floral
decoration, most noticeable in the fabric used to cover the walls or as room
dividers, further unified the decorative scheme. Such touches made it amply
apparent that nature defined the dominant motif. In being as creative as possible
with these complete room ensembles, Lauro and his team of craftsmen
established a paradigm for the Stile Floreale.

Several critics were unsupportive of Lauro's efforts, despite his refined
vision of the truly modern house and the numerous collaborators who
contributed to the collective impact of the palazzina. Even the jury's statement
which accompanied the official gold medal pointed out the problems inherent in

the decorative scheme.[41] The award, repeated below, was presented to Lauro more for effort than for overall result. Their criticisms, however, are difficult to assess since so many of the pieces of furniture have disappeared, and nothing remains of the design program Lauro's firm created.

> Agostino Lauro   Decorator (sic!)
> Awarded gold medal
> We are in the presence of a prizewinner and a prize which clearly require the jury to offer a clarification. No one should have the misleading impression that we admired the Palazzina Lauro with an easy conscience, rising as it is next to and partially emulating the Austrian pavilion.
> Nonetheless, the jury cannot fail to show some appreciation for the first attempt in Italy, in a public exhibition, on a subject of vital importance to modern art. Nor can we ignore the intention. The fact that he has brought together artists, designers, good craftsmen, and shrewd industrialists who have won prizes on their own (and) treated with respect, fully and factually, the intentions of this Exposition, that alone served to ingratiate him to the jury.
> Nevertheless, this prize is not to be interpreted as being offered for all the above efforts. It also was not awarded for the whole work, but rather for some parts of it only.
> For instance, the furniture for the dining room, more modern than new, displays a fine sensibility to constructive line, at any rate, revealing the great assimilative faculty of the artist who designed it. However, the workmanship could have been less hurried, less uncertain, less superficial.
> The same can be said about the salon and the upper bedroom, which has an alcove more suitable for a fashionable goddess of frivolity than the nest of Hymen. The quality of the designer is more distinguished than that of the craftsman. Beautiful and well applied are the fabrics by Pasquina, particularly in a chair in the style of Berlepsch, made for the queen mother (and) done with marguerites on a luminous blue ground.
> Considerable also are the passementeries of Mayno and Deglio, but in poor decorative style are the cushions on the sofas and chairs.
> So this villa is a compendium of mistakes and great successes.
> In awarding this prize we may have exalted the good points more than they deserve in homage to our program and may have overlooked the errors that were in evidence.[42]

Lauro's response to this mixed review is not known. The fact that none of the room interiors has been located suggests that few were saved or purchased after the exhibition closed. No documentary evidence, such as sales records of the Turin exhibition, chronicles what happened to a majority of the furniture, which could have been acquired by wealthy visitors. Only a few documented works that were both shown at the Turin exposition and housed in Lauro's palazzina have been discovered. Additionally, the passage of time has not been kind to Lauro's reputation. Until now, his creative effort at Turin has remained largely unexplored, and his career as a decorator/entrepreneur has gone almost unrecorded.

28 Agostino Lauro. Preliminary drawing for
two sections of the room interior at
Sordevolo, ca. 1900-01. Courtesy: Mitchell
Wolfson Jr. Collection. Cat. no. 8.

29 Agostino Lauro. Preliminary drawing for
sections of the room interior and a major
piece of furniture at Sordevolo, ca. 1900-
01. Courtesy: Mitchell Wolfson Jr. Collection. Cat. no. 9.

THE CONTRIBUTION OF AGOSTINO LAURO TO THE STILE FLOREALE

Despite the partial castigation of the palazzina, the uncanny ability of Agostino
Lauro (1861-1924) to improvise and work with an array of craftsmen under the con-
stant pressure of deadlines is quite remarkable. Lauro demonstrated that Italy
could indeed fashion its own version of the modern townhouse. Even by the
1890s, Lauro had developed an excellent reputation as an entrepreneur and a
designer, which brought him an impressive series of private commissions and
opportunities to decorate official buildings in Turin. Honored during his lifetime,
Lauro frequently introduced his designs at major expositions and operated a
well-known furniture gallery, which may also have housed his workshops, on the
via Genoa in Turin. Distinguished clients were attracted to his showrooms both
before and after the Turin exposition of 1902.[43]

A series of preliminary drawings for a ``double parlor'' or salon (figs. 27-30),
dated April 1900, implies that at the very time of the Paris Exposition Universelle,
Lauro was already at work on advanced, Italian home environments. One draw-

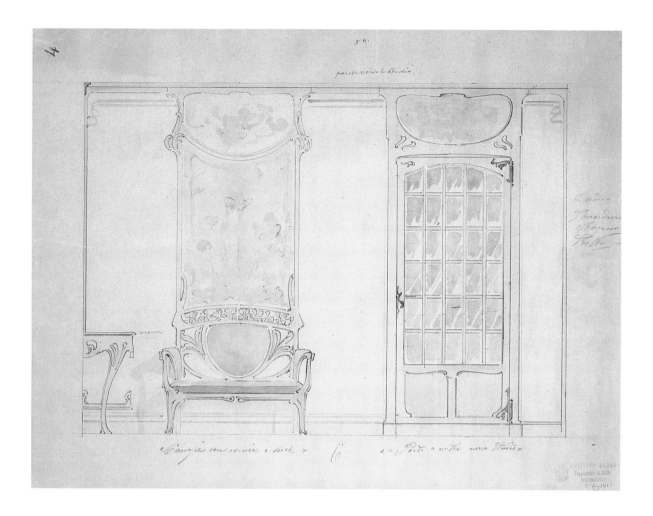

ing (fig. 27), found in its original tube, bears a handwritten inscription that relates
to the construction of a double parlor (fig. 31) for a site near Turin.[44] This completed double parlor was eventually found in a villa in Sordevolo (figs. 31-33), which
indicates that modern interiors were in demand close to the time of the Turin exposition of 1902.[45] Adding to the significance of this commission is the
inclusion of several of the double-parlor chairs (fig. 34) in documentary photographs from the Turin exposition (fig. 35).[46] For this reason, the room interior
stands out not only as an existing example of Lauro's work but also as a reflection
of his productive effort on the various interiors of the palazzina.

A number of issues endure that cannot be easily resolved without additional documentation and investigation. For instance, the mere existence of the
double parlor implies Lauro's satisfaction with this particular room and the initial
success of its installation. The very fact that chairs from the suite were included
in the Turin exposition confirms the value Lauro placed on them, for they fulfilled
the aesthetic requirements of a home environment completed in the ``modern

style." Their identification as major examples by Lauro – they bear his firm's mark on their bases (fig. 36) – attests to their importance at the 1902 Turin exposition.[47] What remains unclear is whether or not this specific interior was installed in a private home prior to 1902. Perhaps it was part of the palazzina's room ensembles and was transported to its intended site only after the Turin showing. Furthermore, since this double parlor had been commissioned prior to 1902, the possibility exists, however unlikely, that a second version was created for use at Turin.

Whichever scenario is favored, the furniture as well as the entire room suite were a known commission by 1902. Originally developed in mid-1900 or 1901, the double parlor might also have contributed to Lauro's esteem as a leader in Italian design reform, which would elevate him to the position of the most likely candidate to construct the palazzina successfully. The room's interior reflected more than Lauro's commitment to international design sources. It demonstrated that he had abandoned historical styles, an attitude then of critical significance in Italy, and had thrown aside the oppressive shackles of eclecticism to create an interior space approaching the organic. Cognizant of French and Belgian sources, Lauro molded forms and manipulated materials to produce visually harmonious environments that followed the dictates of the budding Italian Stile Floreale.

Although destined for a villa ostensibly constructed in the Italian Renaissance/Romanesque revival style, the room reflects the contemporary owners' desire to modify the look of their living environment to match current tastes and fashions. They wanted a living space that stylistically moved away from an idolization of the past, yet at the same time mirrored their substantial wealth. From examining the preliminary drawings, the double parlor originally consisted of twenty-four pieces of furniture, with chairs and bookcases, and heavy wood paneling on a few of the walls. A silk moiré covered with floral motifs identical to that found on the independent chairs adorned other walls. This luxurious material is highly suggestive of Liberty fabrics, then imported into Italy from the well-stocked emporium in London.[48]

As it is now installed, the interior ensemble projects a number of characteristics demanded by Italian designers eager to formulate a new style. The bookcases, complemented by built-in chairs, formed a reading nook that extended from the wall. This type of architectural feature had proven popular in England and Scotland, and examples of it were displayed at the Turin exposition of 1902. Tall backed chairs provided places where occupants could find a moment's repose alone in the small enclave of an organized, controlled space. A similar type of built-in chair environment was incorporated into the palazzina's dining room.[49] (Since floral and vine motifs were combined in the elaborate stained glass windows of the palazzina dining room, Lauro apparently wanted to integrate the furniture with the window treatment and wall surfaces, thus creating a sense of organic intertwining. This same effect is suggested in the double parlor.)

34 Agostino Lauro. Armchair. Carved
mahogany with green silk moiré fabric,
ca. 1900-01. Courtesy: Mitchell Wolfson Jr.
Collection. Cat. no. 13.

37 Agostino Lauro. Detail of wall section from double parlor. Carved mahogany, ca. 1900-01. Courtesy: Mitchell Wolfson Jr. Collection.

35 Agostino Lauro. Diverse furniture at the Turin exposition of 1902. From *I Mobili alla Prima Esposizione Internazionale d'Arte Decorativa Moderna*, Turin, 1902.

36 Agostino Lauro. Detail of maker's stamp on underside of chair, ca. 1900-01. Courtesy: Mitchell Wolfson Jr. Collection.

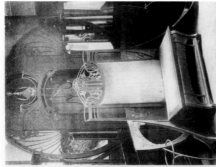

Like the individual pieces of furniture, the side walls of the room ensemble were decorated either with the moiré material or with an elaborate use of wood inlays (fig. 37) set in a swirling, curvilinear pattern to imitate vines and tendrils. In several places, the wooden supports in the room's corners and in the divider between the two sections of the parlor formed stylized supports that held up an illusionary ``outdoor'' wooden trellis (fig. 38) that covered the ceiling. The room interior further assumed the appearance of an outdoor arbor when the linen fabric that covered this trellis was painted with flower and vine designs. Illusion and artifice played a significant role in the final look of this interior. It reinforced one of the fundamental design concerns of the period: the integration of natural motifs with new materials.

To divide the two sections of the double parlor into distinct segments, Lauro constructed a wooden partition with a broad opening for traffic. Clearly, Lauro intended each zone to function independently. The pieces of furniture placed on either side of the partition may have originally bolstered this effect.[50] Yet only the lower area, up to the wainscoting level, suggested that this was a solid partition. The area above the wainscoting was open, with the supporting struts arched to convey a sense of weightlessness and upward mobility. At their pinnacles, the

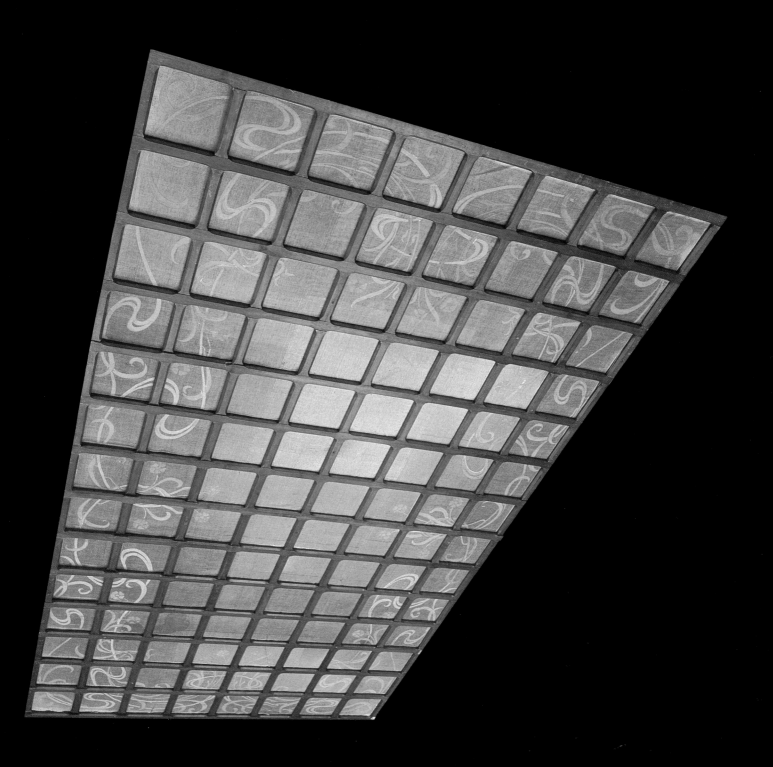

38 Agostino Lauro. Ceiling trellis from the double parlor. Painted linen and wood, ca. 1900-01. Courtesy: Mitchell Wolfson Jr. Collection.

struts formed arches and turned into spandrels (fig. 39) attached to the ceiling,
which provided additional support for the illusionistic wooden trellis and its linen
covering.

In the middle of each spandrel, on both sides of the opening between the
parlor areas, the designer attached metal leaves and chestnuts (fig. 40). These
details heightened the illusion that the vines moved upward along the
architectural members, an effect intensified by the angular, curving metal vines
that jutted into space at the top of each element. The flowering part of each tendril
held an electric light socket. Although he partly hid the light bulbs in the tendrils'
buds, this effort did represent Lauro's attempt to incorporate the newest modes
of lighting into his scheme. It also emphasized his mastery of materials, which
tended to eliminate the long-standing boundaries between the traditional and
the experimental.

Moving away from the central room divider to the corner of the furthermost room, a doorway originally led to an adjoining room. Not intended to strengthen the barrier between one architectural space and the next, this narrow opening was covered with a translucent curtain that allowed light to filter in from another part of the villa. The mahogany wood on either side of the opening repeated the curvilinear pattern of the central partition. Instead of tendrils ending with an attenuated flourish over the doorway, as first intended, a slightly more controlled, curtained valance accented with metal leaves and a chestnut cluster was developed (fig. 41). The same green moiré used on the furniture unified the decorative theme of the walls. Abstractions from nature were elegantly transposed into undulating motifs of wood and metal. In this way, Lauro revealed his keen awareness of the continental art nouveau style, especially that of Belgium.

41 Agostino Lauro. Curtain valance. Green silk moiré fabric lined with brushed cotton, with decorative trim, ca. 1900-01. Courtesy: Mitchell Wolfson Jr. Collection.

42 Agostino Lauro. Parlor table. Carved mahogany, ca. 1900-01. Courtesy: Mitchell Wolfson Jr. Collection. Cat. no. 14.

43 Agostino Lauro. Rectangular table (desk/game table). Carved mahogany with green velvet inset, ca. 1900-01. Courtesy: Mitchell Wolfson Jr. Collection. Cat. no. 15.

Aside from the wood paneling and the silk moiré wall coverings, the individual pieces of furniture elicited the most favorable comments for Lauro's decorative vision. Each example, from the elegant parlor table with a chestnut leaf motif (fig. 42) to a desk or game table (fig. 43), shown in Lauro's display at the Turin exposition (fig. 44), affirmed how furniture could be placed within the double parlor to enhance formality or relaxation. Guests could either play cards, enjoy an after-dinner drink, or simply chat. Different aspects of Italian social mores, depending on the occasion and the nature of the gathering, could be accommodated by the type of furniture and room molding employed (figs. 45, 46).

In one instance, documentation traces the change from what was originally projected (fig. 28) to what was finally installed. Perhaps as late as 1901, Lauro wanted to create a wall niche where a chair or sofa could be secured to the wood paneling. Current reconstruction of the room interior, however, shows no sign of

45 Agostino Lauro. Sofa. Carved mahogany
with green silk moiré fabric, ca. 1900-01.
Courtesy: Mitchell Wolfson Jr. Collection.
Cat. no. 16.

44 Agostino Lauro. Table and chair, Turin, 1902. From *I Mobili alla Prima Esposizione Internazionale d'Arte Decorativa Moderna,* Turin, 1902.

46 Agostino Lauro. Love seat. Carved mahogany with green silk moiré fabric, ca. 1900-01. Courtesy: Mitchell Wolfson Jr. Collection. Cat. no. 17.

50 Agostino Lauro. Detail of love seat. Courtesy: Mitchell Wolfson Jr. Collection. Cat. no. 17.

47 Agostino Lauro. Corner wall section.
Carved mahogany with green silk moiré
fabric, ca. 1900-01. Courtesy: Mitchell
Wolfson Jr. Collection.

49 Agostino Lauro. Side chair. Carved
mahogany with green silk moiré fabric,
ca. 1900-01. Courtesy: Mitchell Wolfson Jr.
Collection. Cat. no. 20.

48 *(Right)* Agostino Lauro. Cabinet (vitrine).
Carved mahogany and beveled glass with
brass mounts, ca. 1900-01. Courtesy:
Mitchell Wolfson Jr. Collection. Cat. no. 19.

such a built-in niche. Only the location of the corner sofas with a carved wall
section (fig. 47) suggests this detail. It remains unclear why this built-in sitting
area was not included in the final version, although it does seem to be the most
prominent modification carried out by Lauro and his wealthy client. Federico
Vercelloni, the owner of the villa, may have wanted greater freedom to move
individual units. Perhaps he preferred not to be tied to the rigid formalization
practiced in the English arts and crafts tradition, the ultimate source for this type
of proposed detail.

With the exception of the ornate cabinet (fig. 48) noted in an early
preliminary drawing, the furniture used throughout the double parlor was not
incorporated into the sketches. In fact, the furniture, which included a chair (fig.
49) and a love seat (fig. 50), might not have been unique pieces designed solely
for the villa at Sordevolo. Detailed business records for Lauro's firm at this period
have not been located, so it is impossible to determine how many of these pieces
were made for or purchased by clients. The possiblity does exist that the tables

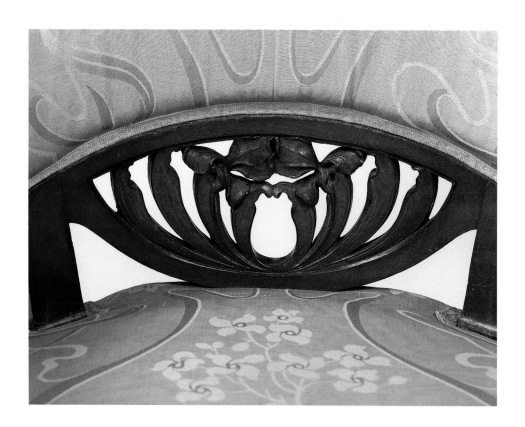

and chairs were part of a popular line of furniture that would have related well
with interiors with corresponding decorative motifs (fig. 51). Indeed, they may
have been mass-produced pieces that even allowed subtle variations in
upholstering. These pieces, which also bear the stenciled mark of Lauro's firm on
their bases, further testify to the Italian designer's talents as an upholsterer and
a decorator. Despite their original purpose, the inclusion of the chair and sofa in
the Turin exposition evinces their importance (fig. 52). It also implies that these
models were still in production in 1902 and were available for purchase (fig. 53).[51]

The richly embellished cabinet (fig. 48), however, truly demonstrates the
technical skill of Lauro's workshops. Even in the preliminary drawings of the
interior (fig. 29), this piece was obviously considered significant. Little about it
changed when it was manufactured for the villa at Sordevolo. In contemporary
photographs of the way pieces were finally arranged inside the double parlor, the
vitrine exudes a sense of distinction. Decorative motifs used throughout the

54 Agostino Lauro. Top of cabinet, ca. 1900-
01. Courtesy: Mitchell Wolfson Jr. Collection. Cat. no. 19.

54 Agostino Lauro. Top of cabinet, ca. 1900-
01. Courtesy: Mitchell Wolfson Jr. Collection. Cat. no. 19.

55 Agostino Lauro. Detail of carved decoration at top of cabinet, ca. 1900-01. Courtesy: Mitchell Wolfson Jr. Collection. Cat. no. 19.

room were crystallized in this single object. The whiplash curve of French art nouveau was combined with the naturalistic floral detailing so central to the Italian Stile Floreale. Leafy curves lead to the precisely rendered flowers of the vitrine's apex (figs. 54, 55). In the curved area beneath the doors (fig. 56) are further references to chestnuts and leaves, underscoring the fundamental leitmotif that runs throughout the interior's decorative detailing. Supports at the base and top also reinforce the relationship between the cabinet and the room's wood paneling.

One unresolved issue prevails: were actual pieces from Sordevolo included in the Turin exposition? Documentary photographs of the exposition present a number of room ensembles and furniture samples Lauro created (fig. 57). Some of these interiors were undoubtedly related to the palazzina. Considering the way illustrations were laid out in the furniture volume *I Mobili* (1902), pieces from the

56 Agostino Lauro. Detail of the carved
chestnut decoration on front of cabinet,
ca. 1900-01. Courtesy: Mitchell Wolfson Jr.
Collection. Cat. no. 19.

Sordevolo villa could have been positioned either inside the Italian pavilion or near the palazzina. Although some furniture textiles differ (fig. 58), the design of the models corresponds with those photographed in 1902, which suggests that others valued Lauro's creations as well. The vitrine, centered in one of these photographs, was included among Lauro's most accomplished works. Already installed in Sordevolo, Lauro may have transported it to Turin or displayed another version of it at the exposition.

Either way, the Sordevolo furniture, if not the entire room itself, was appreciated both as an important example of Lauro's craftsmanship and as a noteworthy contribution to the Stile Floreale. Through this commission, Lauro emerged as an outstanding leader of the design revolution. And Sordevolo, with its magnificent double parlor, became a successful model for private patronage supporting this new decorative style.

57 Agostino Lauro. Furniture at the Turin
exposition of 1902. From *I Mobili alla
Prima Esposizione Internazionale d'Arte
Decorativa Moderna*, Turin, 1902.

OTHER EXHIBITORS IN THE ITALIAN SECTION AT TURIN, 1902

A comprehensive study of the Italian participants in the Turin exposition has not been attempted. Existent documents, essentially archival photographs of buildings and some furniture ensembles, intimate that the exposition included a broad range of ceramics and furniture designs.[52] Since Italian designers had long been interested in the craftsmanship of an object, many of them were exceptionally well trained in molding and decorating materials. A number of commercial design firms in Turin and Milan were eager to establish the modern idiom in home decoration by advancing their own model room suites in the "new style." Some of these furniture ensembles, photographed in situ, were popularized after the exhibition through expansive books and press commentary.

Unfortunately, locating specific suites has proven a difficult undertaking. Much of the furniture has virtually disappeared. Several pieces most likely ended up in country villas, where they were eventually worn by time and use or were replaced to keep up with current fashions. This unavailability of actual objects has made assessing contemporary reviews in the daily press and in monthly journals much more problematic. Without the pieces themselves, comparative evaluations between suites or groups of designers are greatly hindered.

In the case of Vittorio Valabrega, a major contributor to the 1902 exposition, some of his samples from Turin have recently been located. These examples, shown as part of the general Italian section of the exposition and not within the palazzina, form an excellent gauge by which to measure general Italian furniture design with the controversy that surrounded Lauro's palazzina.

Valabrega's long history in the manufacturing of furniture began when he and his brother organized a family firm in the 1800s that specialized in producing highly eclectic pieces based on past period styles. The award of a bronze medal at the Turin exhibition of 1884 confirmed his company's professionalism and attracted clients interested in well-crafted but traditional furniture. As the passion for home decorating escalated during the 1890s, the firm increased in size, with more than fifty craftsmen specializing in woodworking, upholstery, and highly finished objects. By 1898, at the time of the significant decorative arts exhibition in Turin, Valabrega tried to move away from eclecticism by creating a small salon in the Stile Floreale. The press commented upon this room as being the only interior completed in the "new style."

> The walls are covered with olive green moiré, at the top (of which) is a band of embroidered flowers and butterflies, and baseboards in wood. Directly on the green background are three strips of wrought iron intertwined with shapes of leaves that emerge from the corners. . . . On the left and right of the beautiful fireplace, completed in varnished wood, are wrought iron decorations in floral shapes surrounded by polychrome lamps. The light sofa and other chairs and screen are also in green moiré, beautifully embroidered

59 Vittorio Valabrega. Dining room table and chairs. Carved walnut with leather and brass, ca. 1902. Courtesy: Mitchell Wolfson Jr. Collection. Cat. nos. 37, 38.

60 *(Right)* Vittorio Valabrega. Contro-credenza for dining room. Carved walnut with chromed metal mounts, glass, and marble, ca. 1902. Courtesy: Mitchell Wolfson Jr. Collection. Cat. no. 39.

with lilies and poppies in lovely colors. . . . The whole effect is one of lightness, fluency, and elegance; (it is) the perfect setting for the delicate figure of a graceful, blonde lady.[53]

Extremely novel was the use of wrought iron decorations. This trend revealed a new willingness to mix media within a single interior, and Valabrega received a silver medal for his effort.

At the Paris Exposition Universelle of 1900, Valabrega, now a true representative of the new style, was awarded a gold medal, which again called attention to his work and the place he occupied in Italian design reform. A wide range of furniture suites displayed in Turin in 1902 led to his receipt of a silver medal at the First International Exposition of Modern Decorative Art. Even though Valabrega did not receive as much critical attention as Agostino Lauro or Carlo Bugatti, a number of Italian and international critics praised his furniture. Georg Fuchs, for example, linked Valabrega to the more distinguished firms that were then capable of producing accomplished pieces.[54] The Valabrega family remained active in furniture design as late as 1948, but they endured severe hardships under the Fascist-Nazi domination of Italy, particularly when Vittorio's son Ernesto was deported to the death camp in Auschwitz.[55]

61 Alberto Issel. Desk. Oak, metal, leather, fabric, and paint, 1902. Courtesy: Mitchell Wolfson Jr. Collection. Cat. no. 32.

Examination of Valabrega's works suggests that some of them could have been gilded or produced in delicate pastel colors. The sofas with built-in mirrors or wall shelves echo innovations associated with continental art nouveau, such as floral decorations on silk coverings or in the back supports of armchairs. A group of furniture for a dining room (figs. 59, 60) substantiate that Valabrega could work within a highly controlled, simplified format reminiscent of Belgian designs in their "honesty" towards materials and abundance of floral details and decorative tendrils. Valabrega's success at the Turin exposition provided an added impetus to the Italian commitment to modern furniture design. His understated objects also balanced some of the more opulent and overdecorated pieces then being widely discussed.

Among the other Italian furniture designers exhibiting at Turin were the firms of Alberto Issel and Giacomo Cometti. As members of an older generation of artisans, Issel and Cometti had already established themselves as independent craftsmen and overseers of substantial workshops. By 1900 Issel's factory employed over seventy artisans, who created "new style" pieces that were often characterized by abundantly carved floral decorations. Since his pieces were expensive to produce, Issel's furniture appealed to collectors of considerable wealth. This caused Alfredo Melani in his critique of the 1902 Turin exposition to chide Issel gently for creating "seigniorial rooms."

Shipbuilders numbered among Issel's clients. Their commissions may account for his use of nautical motifs, combined with a profuse study of plants, on desks for libraries, for instance (fig. 61). His more advanced and subtly designed chairs and sofas (fig. 62) often employed angular lines, possibly derived from the work of Charles Rennie Mackintosh or the English arts and crafts tradition. Recognized at the Turin exhibition of 1898 and the 1900 Paris Exposition Universelle, Issel's simplified forms made him one of the more internationally astute designers active in Italy at the turn of the century.

Similar to Issel's creations but even more advanced theoretically was the work of Giacomo Cometti, a designer who came late to the applied arts following a career as a sculptor. At the Paris exhibition of 1900, Cometti received an honorable mention for a room interior. Two years later at Turin he was awarded a diploma of honor in humanities. The citation notes his

> intelligent sense of form and workmanship that shows great conscientiousness, intense study, and reiterated reasoning leading to the execution and invention of truly modern furniture. We can use the word artist in the truest sense because Cometti – a sculptor and creator of successful work – has evoked that same spirit in the exercise of decorative, industrial art, becoming a true apostle of modern art. ...
>
> In the construction of his furniture, the artist deserts the sculptural tendency and becomes a follower of forms reminiscent of Nordic countries' design. This is expressed in the logic and continuity of construction. ... He refuses all facile, vulgar forms that are lucrative and only produced to please the uncultivated masses.[56]

62 Alberto Issel. Angled sofa. Oak with
upholstery, 1902. Courtesy: Mitchell
Wolfson Jr. Collection. Cat. no. 34.

Cometti, recognized in 1902 as an artist anxious to create with only the purest of forms, was criticized by some for being too heavily indebted to German designers. Others, especially Alfredo Melani, regarded him as a supreme "rationalist," whose work appeared too simplistic and geometric for many Italian critics. According to the international panel of jurors and the citation given to him, however, Cometti was viewed as a proponent of extreme modernism. The chairs, tables, and vitrines (figs. 63-65) he exhibited in 1902 illustrate his tendency towards streamlined forms. As an independent artist, Cometti voiced further international considerations in Italy and encouraged his fellow designers to examine Germanic and Nordic prototypes as sources for less elaborate interiors.[57]

AN EVALUATION OF THE TURIN EXPOSITION OF 1902 AND THE STILE FLOREALE

Considerable attention was focused on international and native furniture makers in 1902. Critics and supporters of avant-garde modernism seemed to realize that the movement towards visually unified home interiors would certainly fail without the concerted effort and creativity of designers who invented new systems as they remained "honest" in their use of materials. They endorsed interiors filled with light that also used delicate, harmonious colors and simplified shapes. For these reasons, room models exhibitied at Turin were closely scrutinized.

The sheer intensity of the criticism leveled against Italian efforts in furniture design was somewhat unexpected. Some critics apparently sensed that an aura of opportunism, rather than an era of sincere experimentation, prevailed. Alfredo Melani, writing in May of 1902, shortly after the exhibition opened, summed up one reaction to the situation.

> We would do ourselves harm if we did not acknowledge that, in general, Italy is poorly represented at the Exhibition in Turin. The most pleasant impression received when visiting the exhibited works is that the period of aesthetic servility is ceasing in our country, which has joined the others on the field of new activity. However, this impression refers to the classification of many works, especially with regard to furniture.[58]

Melani continued his examination of the pieces by stressing that modern art must follow an ethically moral path if works "sincere" in their implications were to be created. To him, the idea that some designs emphasized a manipulation of materials simply grated against the aesthetic code of the avant-garde.

> However, how many craftsmen and designers at the exhibition are sincere? I may be mistaken, but I believe that the fingers on one hand will be sufficient to count them all. Moreover, the vast majority of Italian exhibitors produce Art Nouveau because it is a good time for this type of art. But then, what is Art Nouveau? The exhibitors copy modern objects from books and magazines just as they earlier copied ancient objects from books and magazines. Very

few suspect the existence of modern idealism, are capable of emotions, or are adept at giving the image of an honest vision.

This is the painful truth, which is good for us Italians to recognize before others confirm our superficiality once more. All this is the effect of superficiality, more than the result of influence exercised by our own traditions. It is often said that we, the Italians, are the least inclined to receive and produce Art Nouveau because the old national traditions, especially classical traditions, oppress our spirit. This is an uncontestable truth, but all this could be corrected given an education that is not exclusively formal in nature.[59]

Intended to strike aesthetic nerves, Melani's comments pushed Italian designers away from a mere manual understanding of the "new style" towards the creation of forms based on an honest interaction with materials. The critic sensed that Italian designers had based their variation of art nouveau not on moral consciousness or a true understanding of the implications and goals of international design reform, but on commercial necessity. To meet the demands of clients, they simply produced versions of European prototypes. Melani continued:

An important manufacturer confessed to me that he would abandon Art Nouveau if the furniture he exhibited, inspired by an apparent aesthetic freedom, remained for the most part unsold. In fact, manufacturers have the need to sell; but even among artists, faith is obscured by opportunism. This provides a rationale to the enemies of our sweet idealism, those who think that Art Nouveau is a transitory form because it has no deep roots in the person who produces it.

It is true; this is not faith. Among the Italians in the Exhibition of Turin, those of us who beat the path of our art keep contending in vain with the knowledge that we are performing a beautiful and daring act. Before there are works, it is necessary to create a conscience. I prefer men who hurl against Art Nouveau the most bestial accusations to men who surround it with interested caresses. The latter are the worst enemies of present idealism: they would injure it if it were so tenuous as to dissolve at the slightest touch. Thus, they slow down the triumph of modern aesthetic thought, and countries that have already changed years ago will wonder increasingly at Italian insensibility.[60]

Continually aware that a pure form of Stile Floreale had to be nurtured, Melani called for apostles of modernism in Italy to develop aesthetic theories in a more vigorous manner. This tactic was similar to the way critics and aestheticians in other countries had urged the creation of an art nouveau style. Without such confrontation, which Melani thoroughly expected to foster with his public criticism, outsiders would persist in viewing Italy as asleep and unable to collect her thoughts.

At the same time he penned these cautionary statements, Melani was clever enough to enumerate the heroes of "true modernism" he observed at the Turin exposition. His failure to do this might have suggested that all Italian efforts in furniture making had been in vain.

> The artist who knows how to give a truly individual imprint to his furniture is C. Bugatti. Not everything that flows from the fantasy of this Milanese artist is beautiful. His work as a whole seems to be a reflection of oriental fantasies. ... This is why Bugatti, living outside every movement and owing everything to himself and demanding everything from himself, is nevertheless the exhibitor who most clearly remains stamped in one's memory.[61]

In addition to the considerable praise Bugatti received, Melani pointed out the individualistic efforts of Eugenio Quarti, who ``works artistically without changing

the day after, driven by gusts of profit." Melani was also inspired by the work of the "strong and independent manufacturer," Carlo Zen.

While the critic found much to admire in these men – although he mysteriously failed to comment on Lauro or Valabrega – Melani remained extremely fearful that enticing commercialism might prove too pervasive to allow the eventual triumph of creativity and imagination.

> The commercial current invades (creativity) from one end to the other, and the shareholders with their own demands side with those who buy, namely, the general public, and not with those who feel, the artists. Accordingly, in a moment like this, while the struggle between the old and the new is continuous, tenacious, and pressing, the manufacturing establishment cannot side with the innovators who represent the minority. The situation will be resolved when everybody belongs to the minority.[62]

In the end, Melani agreed that there were many "interesting" currents within the art nouveau/Stile Floreale idiom, simply because it was topical and timely. Nevertheless, it would remain for history to assess what was most original in the Italian section at Turin. As he awaited this evaluation, Melani never foresaw that the "new style" would be superseded by other trends, ones that would relegate all efforts at the turn of the century to relative obscurity. Melani could not identify, despite a perceptive eye, all the modernist efforts on view at Turin in 1902.

The enthusiasm generated by Melani's early rush to designate the leaders of modernism at Turin was tempered when, at the close of the exposition six months later, another critic, U. Fleres, countered that it was not "easy to assess ... significance."[63] Perhaps somewhat reluctantly, however, Fleres did reconfirm that the exposition had indeed inspired a new style. This aesthetic development, he ventured, could be labeled "floral or even Liberty," although it was still a style that had to be characterized and situated within a fixed historical continuum. Fleres then added his own note of caution: Stile Floreale itself would soon be surpassed by another. Once a style became dominant, other movements surfaced in reaction to it, thus initiating the process anew. In a sense, Fleres anticipated the historical reconsideration of Stile Floreale that goes on today.

The main practitioners of Stile Floreale in architecture continue to be discovered, while those whose work led toward an Italian art nouveau in furniture and interior design are now the subject of critical reappraisal. A sign of the seriousness of this endeavor is how the Stile Floreale period, now considered to extend from about 1898 to the early years of World War I (ca. 1914), has been examined and expanded. Students of this particular phase of modern design reform now conclude that Italy did achieve, albeit modestly, a measure of innovation based on individualistic principles rather than on slavish imitation of the past. Scrutinizing later variants of Stile Floreale and how natural motifs were utilized in other countries demonstrates the complexity of this design tradition.

PART II: THE CULT OF NATURE MAINTAINED

THE STILE FLOREALE: ITALY FROM TURIN TO WORLD WAR I

Despite the often perceived collapse of the art nouveau style after the Turin exposition of 1902, design reform subsequently took hold in Italy. It produced a lasting effect on the more progressive creators of the time. Carlo Zen maintained his prominence by manufacturing furniture based on art nouveau and symbolist motifs that appealed primarily to feminine tastes. His inlaid mother-of-pearl designs along the border of a curio cabinet (figs. 66-69) further refined details he had first utilized on pieces shown in 1902. His inlays became more geometric closer to the end of the first decade of the twentieth century. For example, the fluid outline of a grandfather clock (figs. 70, 71) shows a heightened simplification of Austrian and German forms. Zen, who understood how the Stile Floreale could be influenced and nurtured by foreign designs, remained one of the more skillful Italian manufacturers of the twentieth century.

Also dominating this phase of the Stile Floreale was the firm of Ernesto Basile and Vittorio Ducrot. In a 1903 secretary (figs. 72, 73), completed in carved, painted, and gilded mahogany, they revealed their own awareness of continental sources, yet their lingering advocacy of a floral style is most notable in the metal fittings. A somewhat archaic derivation of the art nouveau aesthetic is pronounced in a rocking chair by Basile (figs. 74, 75). Here, symbolist details and an interest in nature fuse. The whiplash motifs of the arms, combined with the implied movement of the chair, indicate that Basile had mastered the curvilinear rhythms of international art nouveau.

Similarly, Eugenio Quarti continued to produce exquisite pieces of wood furniture with details of brass, copper, and silver wire, and inlays of mother-of-pearl. Delicate chairs (fig. 76) designed for a salon convey a sense of wealth and ornate splendor quite fitting for their intended owners. Since these chairs were also displayed at the Paris Exposition Universelle of 1900, they attested to Quarti's worldwide reputation as a designer of furniture and entire room ensembles (fig. 77). Quarti practiced this refined type of decoration as late as 1908 or 1910, as a jewelry box adorned with abstract patterns of mother-of-pearl inlays verifies (fig. 78).

68 Carlo Zen. Detail of curio cabinet, with
  sunburst design in brass and gold leaf,
  ca. 1902. Courtesy: Mitchell Wolfson Jr.
  Collection. Cat. no. 40.

66 *(Right)* Carlo Zen. Curio cabinet. Mahogany with glass and inlays of brass, mother-of-pearl, and gold leaf, ca. 1902. Courtesy: Mitchell Wolfson Jr. Collection. Cat. no. 40.

69 Carlo Zen. Detail of curio cabinet, ca. 1902. Courtesy: Mitchell Wolfson Jr. Collection. Cat. no. 40.

70 Carlo Zen. Grandfather clock. Fruitwood
   with beveled glass and inlays of brass
   and mother-of-pearl, ca. 1908. Courtesy:
   Mitchell Wolfson Jr. Collection. Cat. no. 41.

74 Ernesto Basile. Rocking chair. Carved
    maple with woven silk upholstery, ca.
    1898-1900. Courtesy: Mitchell Wolfson Jr.
    Collection. Cat. no. 25.

75 Ernesto Basile. Detail of rocking chair, ca.
    1898-1900. Courtesy: Mitchell Wolfson Jr.
    Collection. Cat. no. 25.

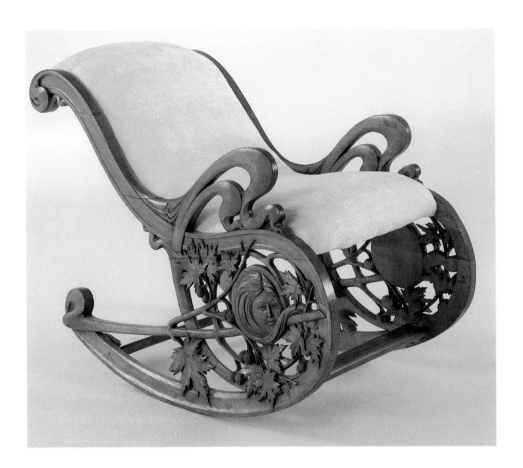

76 Eugenio Quarti. Chair. Mahogany with
   mother-of-pearl inlays; brass, copper, and
   silver wire; and upholstery, ca. 1900.
   Courtesy: Mitchell Wolfson Jr. Collection.
   Cat. no. 35.

Aside from innovations in furniture, one place the Stile Floreale most greatly affected interior design was in the use of ceramic tiling for moldings and room accents, as on fireplace surrounds. The decades immediately before and after the turn of the century can be termed a period of renaissance in ceramic decoration. Motifs used inside (and often on the exterior) of the modern home adopted abstract as well as literal designs from nature. This utilization of recognizable, natural motifs, such as stylized poppies (fig. 79), substantiated that Italian ceramists could indeed create lively, striking forms to complement the modern home. While the precise use and number of this colorful ceramic is not known – it may have been part of an extensive frieze of poppies – it does illustrate how such tiles were successfully integrated into Stile Floreale interiors. A repeated pattern of abstractly rendered natural motifs, quite reminiscent of stems or leaves, appears in a ca. 1910 fireplace surround (fig. 80). Such details carried the revolution in home decoration, now in an abstract style, toward World War I and an era of streamlined design.

79 Galileo Chini for l'Arte della Ceramica.
Tile. Glazed earthenware, ca. 1898-99.
Courtesy: Mitchell Wolfson Jr. Collection.
Cat. no. 27.

80 Galileo Chini for l'Arte della Ceramica. Fireplace surround. Mahogany with glazed earthenware tiles, ca. 1910. Courtesy: Mitchell Wolfson Jr. Collection. Cat. no. 28.

81 Designer unknown, Gorham Silver Company. Container and lid. Sterling silver and other metals, United States, ca. 1881. Courtesy: Mitchell Wolfson Jr. Collection. Cat. no. 45.

82 Designer unknown, Gorham Silver Company. Pitcher. Sterling silver, United States, 1881. Courtesy: Mitchell Wolfson Jr. Collection. Cat. no. 44.

83 Louis Comfort Tiffany as designer and manufacturer. Vase. Glazed earthenware, United States, ca. 1905. Courtesy: Mitchell Wolfson Jr. Collection. Cat. no. 43.

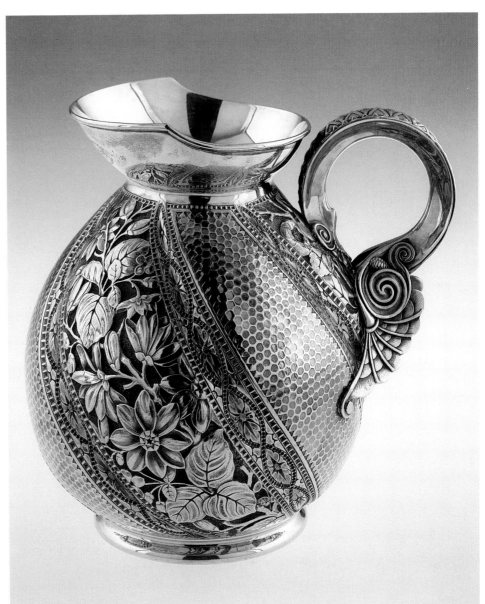

84 J.H. Gest for Baldwin Piano Company.
Piano and bench. Carved, incised, and
painted mahogany, Cincinnati, Ohio,
1904. Courtesy: Mitchell Wolfson Jr. Collection. Cat. no. 42.

THE CULT OF NATURE: UNITED STATES AND ENGLAND

Italy was not the only nation obsessed with nature in design during the closing
years of the nineteenth century. In fact, almost all Western nations were then
investigating similar paths. As early as the 1880s in the United States,
artists/decorators working with exquisitely carved silver containers revealed a
penchant for nature. Whether a spider's web provided naturalistic detail (fig. 81)
or flowers and leaves formed a more stylized pattern on a pitcher or vase (figs. 82,
83), American craftsmen stood at the forefront of the design reform movement.
Many critics of the time noted that Americans had fewer historicisms to eliminate,
so they were able to probe the world with fresh eyes. Progressive American
designers even applied decorations on pianos (figs. 84, 85), mixing naturalistic
description in painted scenes of lakes and mountains with imaginative vegetal
abstractions to create symbolic accents.

At a time when British designers were also breaking with historical styles,
Thomas Jeckyll, an English designer familiar to the painter James Abbott

87 W.A.S. Benson. Firescreen. Copper and brass, England, 1891. Courtesy: Mitchell Wolfson Jr. Collection. Cat. no. 46.

86 Thomas Jeckyll for Barnard, Bishop and Barnard. Fireplace surround. Cast iron with silvered bronze patina, England, 1873. Courtesy: Mitchell Wolfson Jr. Collection. Cat. no. 47.

McNeill Whistler, created a fireplace surround (fig. 86; 1873) with motifs inspired by flowers and Japanese art. Indeed, Japanese medallions and sword-guards, with their own derivations of flowers and animals, furnished Jeckyll with a wealth of designs prime for abstraction. Today, Jeckyll's creations exemplify what took place near the turn of the century when the arts and crafts tradition made exceptional headway in the field of applied arts.

89 Designer unknown. Electric heater. Hammered and pierced copper, and cast iron, Scotland, ca. 1905. Courtesy: Mitchell Wolfson Jr. Collection. Cat. no. 55.

88 W.A.S. Benson. Electric light sconce. Copper and brass with vaseline glass shades, England, 1902. Courtesy: Mitchell Wolfson Jr. Collection.

British mesmerization by the sunflower, a primary symbol of the arts and crafts movement, provided a convenient reference point for W.A.S. Benson in his firescreen (fig. 87) of the early 1890s. Benson's position as a respected practitioner of the arts and crafts tradition, a staunch advocate of honesty in materials, and a major craftsman who closely monitored the artists in his London-based firm allowed him to produce useful objects designed with an eye toward creativity. This firescreen, for example, confirms his ability to abstract from nature. An electric light sconce (fig. 88) dated just after the turn of the century further underlines his predilection for naturalistic design. (The support looks like a plant tendril, and the light sconce suggests a plant bulb.)

By the turn of the century, the same preoccupation with metalwork design had spread to Scotland. The unknown designer of an electric heater (fig. 89) embellished its surface with motifs reminiscent of buds, plants, and miniature trees. These objects not only document Scottish absorption with metalwork but also clearly indicate the commitment of a growing number of artists to the cult of nature.

90 William Morris, and William Morris and Company. Wallpaper sample in a lily, marigold, and bluebonnet pattern. Printed paper, England, designed 1873, manufactured ca. 1880. Courtesy: Mitchell Wolfson Jr. Collection. Cat. no. 48.

91 William Morris, and William Morris and Company. Wallpaper sample in a marigold pattern. Printed paper, England, ca. 1900. Courtesy: Mitchell Wolfson Jr. Collection. Cat. no. 49.

92 William Morris, and William Morris and Company. Wallpaper sample in a honeysuckle pattern. Printed paper, England, ca. 1900. Courtesy: Mitchell Wolfson Jr. Collection. Cat. no. 50.

93 William Morris, and William Morris and Company. Wallpaper sample in a poppy pattern. Printed paper, England, ca. 1900. Courtesy: Mitchell Wolfson Jr. Collection. Cat. no. 51.

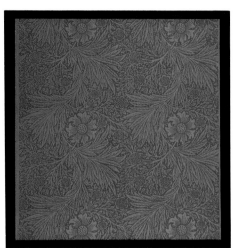

An interest in floral motifs within a repetitive pattern was initiated early, especially in the realm of wallpapers and textiles designed by William Morris and Company (fig. 90). By 1900, Morris explored all-over designs in his wallpaper samples. Vines and tendrils filled the surface (figs. 91-93) to form dense, luxurious patterns. A tulip motif (fig. 94) became one of Morris' best known design concepts. These wallpaper patterns proved popular because they imbued interiors with a sense of liveliness and because they fostered the impression that nature had been used in a way that was not too costly to the contemporary decorator. Similarly, in a curtain panel of ca. 1897 (fig. 95), Charles Voysey combined birds and a fruit tree motif into a stylized pattern that emphasized the two-dimensional quality of the surface.

94 William Morris, and William Morris and Company. Wallpaper sample in a garden tulip pattern. Printed paper, England, ca. 1900. Courtesy: Mitchell Wolfson Jr. Collection. Cat. no. 52.

95 Charles Voysey. Curtain panel. Cotton, Great Britain, ca. 1897. Courtesy: Mitchell Wolfson Jr. Collection. Cat. no. 53.

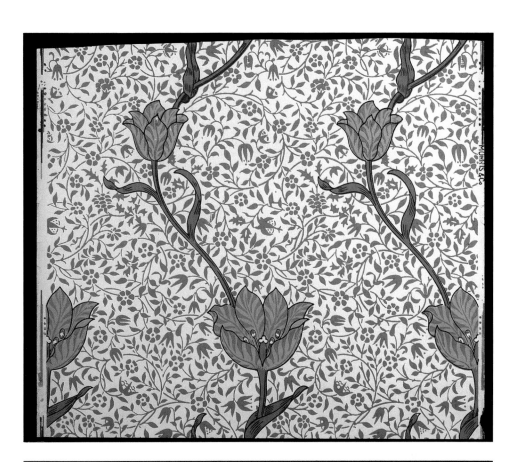

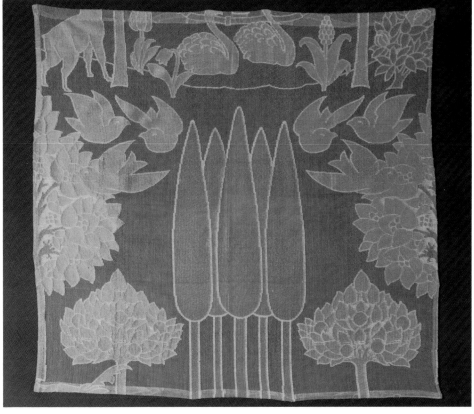

96 V.C. Andreoli for the Rozenburg Factory. Design for a vase: Indian cress. Watercolor and pencil on paper, Holland, ca. 1900. Courtesy: Mitchell Wolfson Jr. Collection. Cat. no. 56.

97 J. Barendsen for the Rozenburg Factory. Design for a vase: tulips. Watercolor and pencil on paper, Holland, ca. 1905. Courtesy: Mitchell Wolfson Jr. Collection. Cat. no. 58.

98 Attributed to J. W. van Rossum for the
Rozenburg Factory. Design for a tableau
of eighty-four tiles with bulbs/flowers.
Watercolor and pencil on paper, Holland,
ca. 1897. Courtesy: Mitchell Wolfson Jr.
Collection. Cat. no. 61.

HOLLAND AND GERMANY

In Holland and Germany, plants and lines were often intertwined in colorful designs on ceramics or tiles. These motifs, developed by the Rozenburg Factory in the Hague, frequently covered an object's surface with a vine pattern to draw attention to the full shape of, perhaps, a vase (figs. 96, 97). Flowers in brilliant colors might also define the starting point of a decorative tile frieze for a home (figs. 98-100). Frequently, natural patterns that bordered on pure abstraction fused a Dutch predilection for Javanese motifs with the craft of batik. Once transferred to ceramic pieces, the unusual color combinations and intensely abstracted design motifs (figs. 101, 102) emerged as among the most startling creations at the turn of the century.

99 Attributed to S. Schellink for the
Rozenburg Factory. Design for a tableau
of thirty-five tiles: foliage. Watercolor and
pencil on paper, Holland, ca. 1897. Courtesy: Mitchell Wolfson Jr. Collection.

100 Attributed to S. Schellink for the
Rozenburg Factory. Design for a tableau
of sixty-six tiles with water lilies. Watercolor and pencil on paper, Holland, ca.
1897. Courtesy: Mitchell Wolfson Jr. Collection. Cat. no. 59.

102 Attributed to W.P. Hartgring. Design for a tableau of fifty tiles with tulip motif. Watercolor and pencil on paper, Holland, ca. 1897. Courtesy: Mitchell Wolfson Jr. Collection.

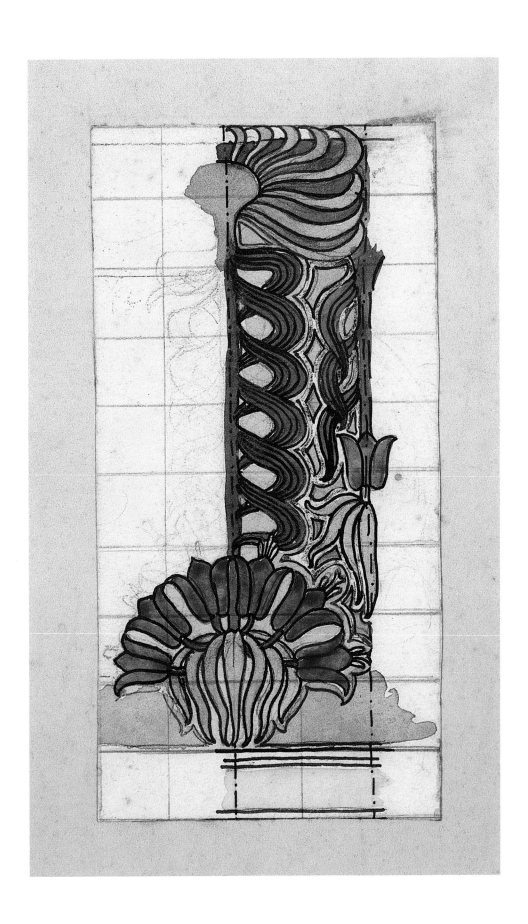

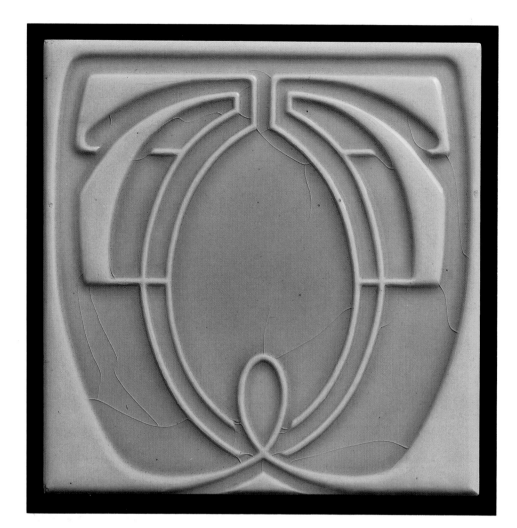

Variations of nature led to increasingly geometric shapes in Germany as well, as a vase by Max Laeuger (fig. 103) and ceramic tiles produced by such leading manufactories as the Villeroy and Boch Mosaikfabrik (figs. 104-106) indicate. This same tendency towards clean lines and simplified forms was employed in ceramic plates by Peter Behrens (figs. 107, 108) and Ferdinand Selle (fig. 109). Only on rare occasions did a sense of organic growth predominate in German porcelains (fig. 110), for German designs usually focused on streamlined, geometric forms instead.

105 Designer unknown for Wessel's
Wandplatten-Fabrik. Tile. Glazed earthenware, Germany, ca. 1902. Courtesy:
Mitchell Wolfson Jr. Collection. Cat. no. 70.

106 Otto Eckmann for Villeroy and Boch
Mosaikfabrik. Tile. Glazed earthenware,
Germany, ca. 1900. Courtesy: Mitchell
Wolfson Jr. Collection. Cat. no. 64.

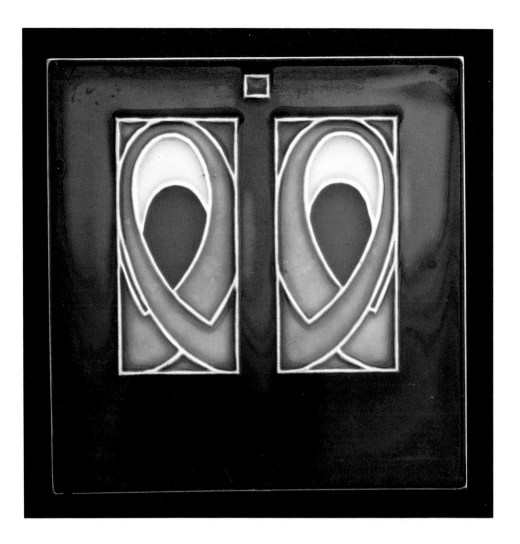

107 Peter Behrens for Porzellanfabrik
Gebrüder Bauscher. Plate. Porcelain, Ger-
many, 1901. Courtesy: Mitchell Wolfson Jr.
Collection. Cat. no. 63.

108 School of Peter Behrens for Krautheim &
Adelberg. Plate. Porcelain, Germany,
1902. Courtesy: Mitchell Wolfson Jr. Collection. Cat. no. 62.

109 Ferdinand Selle for Porzellan Manufaktur-Burgau. Plate. Glazed earthenware, Germany/Austria, ca. 1907. Courtesy: Mitchell Wolfson Jr. Collection. Cat. no. 69.

110 Theo Schmuz-Baudiss for Königliche Porzellan Manufaktur. Vase. Porcelain, Germany, ca. 1895-1900. Courtesy: Mitchell Wolfson Jr. Collection. Cat. no. 68.

FRANCE AND BELGIUM

The impact of nature, also felt in France and Belgium, appeared in different ways. French designers intimately explored all aspects of nature, as animal and plant motifs dominated in furniture and ceramic designs at the end of the century. Occasionally, a designer moved away from recognizable forms to experiment with more organic qualities. These pieces fully synthesized natural motifs with practical shapes, as seen in vases created by the architect Hector Guimard (fig. 111).

In Belgium, Henry van de Velde (figs. 112, 113) investigated abstractions from nature, which he later perfected in Germany after the turn of the century. These utilitarian pieces, with motifs inspired by waves and vines, are among the more perfectly realized examples of nature's influence over design. Yet the most sucessful modern designers were those, such as van de Velde, who reduced

112 Henry van de Velde for Staatliche
Porzellan Manufaktur. Coffeepot and lid.
Porcelain, Germany, ca. 1905. Courtesy:
Mitchell Wolfson Jr. Collection. Cat. no. 72.

113 Henry van de Velde for Staatliche
    Porzellan Manufaktur. Sugar bowl and lid.
    Porcelain, Germany, ca. 1905. Courtesy:
    Mitchell Wolfson Jr. Collection. Cat. no. 73.

obvious references to nature. To this Belgian designer, line ranked supreme. It provided the force and strength of his extraordinary creations.

Decorative design that emphasized form and function emerged triumphant in the simplified, vegetal shapes of objects produced worldwide by 1902-1905. Somewhat later, the Stile Floreale exhibited tendencies similar to those apparent in other countries, especially in Scotland, Germany, and Belgium. Designers from these nations stood at the vanguard of innovation in the early 1900s. Sadly, Italian designers remained in a secondary arena of design reform, despite Italy's golden hopes for further aesthetic development and the numerous awards its artists received for their contributions to the First International Exposition of Modern Decorative Art (fig. 114).

114 Leonardo Bistolfi. Diploma of the *Prima Esposizione Internazionale d'Arte Decorativa Moderna, Torino, 1902 (Diploma di Medaglia d'Oro al Signor J.J. Scharvogel)*, Italy, 1902. Courtesy: Mitchell Wolfson Jr. Collection. Cat. no. 7.

NOTES

1 For reference, see G. Machi, "Esposizione d'Arte Decorativa Moderna, Torino, Italia ed. il estero," in *Il Tempo* (Milan, 7 July 1902), as quoted in Francesca R. Fratini, *Esposizione Torino 1902, Polemiche in Italia sull'Arte Nuova*, 85-86. Italy's relationship in the visual arts with other European countries was tested at the Turin exposition of 1902. This exhibition brought together many different artists/designers through works specifically created for it. Since that time, many of the works have been destroyed or remain unlocated.

2 Even though Liberty and Company was not represented at the Turin exposition of 1902, the shop exerted great influence in Italy by providing one of the alternative names for the new style. For further reference, see Valentino Brosio, *Lo Stile Liberty in Italia*, 36-42.

 To refer to the same decorative arts tradition in Italy, the use of the name Stile Floreale was widespread. The term often appears with architecture and architectural decoration that utilized floral motifs with an increased reliance on nature. For further reference, see Carroll L.V. Meeks, "The Real 'Liberty' of Italy: The Stile Floreale," 113-30. Professor Meeks tried to decipher English influences on Italian architecture by noting the significance of residences "built for prosperous bourgeoisie" as the key area for the full flowering of the Stile Floreale. The organic appearance of some Stile Foreale motifs could have been influenced by the French designer Louis Majorelle. Similar floral qualities are found in the school of furniture decoration emanating from Nancy, France. For further reference, see *Testimonianze Liberty a Genova*, Genoa, 1986.

3 The importance of the Dresden exhibition in fostering design reform and in promoting the utilization of room installations has not been adequately addressed. Brief mention is made in S. Tschudi Madsen, *Sources of Art Nouveau*, 328. Part of the hesitation to investigate Dresden (1897) lies in the difficulty in locating adequate research materials on this exhibition and in determining what may have happened to some of the room interiors shown at the time.

4 For reference to van de Velde at Bing's shop, see Gabriel P. Weisberg, *Art Nouveau Bing: Paris Style 1900*, 70, 82, 84. Van de Velde's rooms seem to have disappeared after being shown in Dresden, suggesting that they were either secured by a collector in Germany or shipped back to Bing for eventual installation elsewhere.

5 Italian ties with the Liberty firm were extensive, although not well documented. Also, the Liberty archives in London were extensively damaged, which impedes precise verification of the international dealers who may have purchased materials for eventual sale in foreign shops. Nothing prevented Italians from ordering directly from Liberty's in London, and this type of direct transaction was never adequately documented. For further suggestions, see Brosio, *Lo Stile Liberty in Italia*, 36-42.

6 For an examination of ties with England, see Meeks, "The Real 'Liberty' of Italy," 118.

7 For reference to Italy at the 1900 Exposition Universelle, see Brosio, *Lo Stile Liberty*, 36-42. Carlo Bugatti and the firms of Vittorio Valabrega in Turin and Eugenio Quarti in Milan were singled out as design leaders. Quarti was actually presented with a major award at the Paris fair, making him the first Italian furniture manufacturer to receive an accomplished award at a significant international exhibition. Many of the other eclectic examples from Italy closely imitated past styles.

8 For reference to the members who composed the Turin jury, see *Relazione della Giuria Internazionale della Prima Esposizione d'Arte Decorativa Moderna*. As president of the jury, Albert Besnard was distinguished for his work in stained glass and room interiors. For further reference to the work of Besnard, see Gabriel P. Weisberg, "Albert Besnard's Portrait of Mme Lerolle and her Daughter Yvonne," *Bulletin of the Cleveland Museum of Art* 64, no. 10 (December 1977): 326-43.

9 See *Relazione*. Teserone and Calandra were the only jury members to represent Italy.

10 *Ibid.*, 12-13.

11 Enrico Thovez, "Cronaca dell'Esposizione Internazionale d'Arte Decorativa Moderna a Torino," in *L'Arte Decorativa Moderna*, 1-3, as quoted in Fratini, *Esposizione*, 139-40. Thovez, a critic, also functioned as the secretary of the "Artistic Committee" for the Turin exposition, which guarantees that his writings carried the sanctions of official pronouncement and an intimate understanding of the designers' goals.

12 *Ibid.*

13 *Ibid.*

14 *Relazione*, 47.

15 *Ibid.*, 51. Objects produced in Bing's ateliers were definitely for sale at the Turin exposition.

16 One of Bing's principal furniture designers, Eugène Gaillard, was not well represented at Turin. Gaillard exhibited chairs and furniture that, according to the catalogue, were "not well chosen." See *Relazione*, 53.

17 Van de Velde was also not well represented at Turin, because he decided to exhibit only "two showcases," which have not been fully identified. Due to this limited representation, the official exhibition jury deemed van de Velde a non-participant. See *Relazione*, 53.

18 *Ibid.*, 111-13.

19 *Ibid.*

20 *Ibid.*, 133.

21 See Georg Fuchs, *Erste Internationale Ausstellung für Moderne Dekorative Kunst in Turin*, 217-24. Fuchs was a widely respected critic, but he maintained a strong Germanic bias that was conditioned by his friendship with Alexander Koch and the creative achievements at Darmstadt.

22 *Ibid.*

23 For further reference, see Walter Crane, "Modern Decorative Art," 488-93.

24 *Ibid.*, 493. This wording suggests that Crane was offended by some of the exaggerated tendencies other international critics noted in the Italian section.

25 Thovez, "Cronaca," 1-3.

26 See Romualdo Pantini, "L'Esposizione di Torino," 2, as quoted in Fratini, *Esposizione*, 256-57.

27 See Efisto Aitelli, "Esposizione Internazionale d'Arte Decorativa Moderna di Torino," 750-62, as quoted in Fratini, *Esposizione*, 268-69.

28 See Vittorio Pica, *L'Arte Decorativa all'Esposizione di Torino del 1902*, 331-78. Pica's text is a very detailed account of each country's major achievements, replete with appropriate photographs from the Turin exposition.

29 *Ibid.*, 373-74. For further attention to furniture, see *I Mobili alla Prima Esposizione*.

30 *Ibid.*, 377-78.

31 *Ibid.*

32 Roger Marx, "L'Exposition internationale d'art décoratif moderne à Turin," 506-10. Marx noted, "Everyone retained a most pitiful memory of the Italian section at the Universal Exhibition of 1900: nothing was worthy of being preserved, and fault could be found in almost everything. . . ."

33 *Ibid.*

34 See *Relazione*, 164.

35 See A. Frizzi, "L'Esposizione Internazionale d'Arte Decorativa Moderna a Torino, 1902: La Villa Lauro," 353-55.

36 *Ibid.*

37 *Ibid.*

38 For reference to Giuseppe Velati-Bellini, see Frank Russell, ed., *Art Nouveau Architecture* (New York: Rizzoli, 1979), 206-7. Also see Mila Leva Pistoi, *Torino Mezzo Secolo di Architettura, 1865–1915*, 214-20.

39 Frizzi, 353-55.

40 *Ibid.*

41 This award is difficult to comprehend. It contains a number of negative comments about the effects of the palazzina, which may have emerged from the international nature of the jury. Perhaps finding themselves in a difficult position and being fully aware of accomplishments in other countries, the jury members could not totally castigate the palazzina, even though they believed many of its decorative elements were imitative. On the other hand, they recognized that Italy had progressed in decorative design since 1900, which they needed to acknowledge.

42 See *Relazione*, 164. It is not known who drafted the text of this award. Since its wording pays extremely close attention to elements of craftsmanship, an artisan may have had a hand in drafting the language that was finally published in the exhibition report.

43 Biographical information on Lauro or details about his decorating firm in Turin are difficult to obtain. What has been located has led to conflicting conclusions about his importance as a designer. Discussions with art historians, art dealers, and Lauro family members have revealed

that assessing Lauro's contributions is tenuous. Much of the work he produced or supervised has been lost or destroyed.

For a brief mention of Lauro, see Irene de Guttry and Maria Paola Maino, *Il Mobile Liberty Italiano,* 164-65. Reproductions of several pieces of his furniture, including some shown in the Turin exposition of 1902, are found in this book.

Other information is contained in *Esposizione Nazionale del 1898* (Turin: Frassati and Company, 1898), 211. Its author notes that "among the decorators who are working in this genre (the modern style) and are exhibiting their work here, top honors, according to the judgment of the intelligentsia, should go to Lauro of Torino."

At the Turin exhibition of 1898, Lauro exhibited three rooms, including a dining room with paneled wood and a bedroom. The furniture was upholstered with Liberty velour, similar to the set Lauro eventually designed for Sordevolo. In fact, some rooms completed for the 1898 exhibition are decidedly forerunners of the private commission for the double parlor.

This article also reveals that Lauro operated a vast workshop, whose chief designer was named Barbasio. It goes on to note that Lauro completed work on a number of private villas and official buildings in Turin, including the Philharmonic Academy. The background of Lauro's early work needs to be investigated more fully to provide specific contexts for these private commissions and for his success at the Turin exposition of 1902.

Some disagreement also exists over Lauro's date of death. His death certificate from the city of Turin states that he died on November 3, 1924. Information in an obituary that appeared in a 1925 issue of the newspaper *Labor* and from the Ministry of *Economia Nazionale* notes that Lauro died one year later, on November 3, 1925. Only an examination of his tombstone in Turin will confirm the exact date of death.

For further archival documentation of Lauro's work, see photograph albums in the Scuola Professionale dei Tappezzieri in Turin. These albums, given to the school by Lauro's wife after his death, provide a visual record of some of the furniture he produced during his career and records other pieces influential to the formation of his taste.

44 This drawing, along with others, was included in the sale of furniture from the double parlor when these pieces were purchased for the Mitchell Wolfson Jr. Collection in Miami, Florida. The inscription reads: "Sketch by Agostino Lauro. To be returned after having served the purpose for the necessary modifications so work can be successfully carried out as conceived and ordered. Turin, April 2, 1900. (Signed) Fed. Vercelloni."

Beyond establishing an accurate date for the production of the double parlor, this

inscription raises other issues. 1.) Lauro's sketch may have been made to clarify necessary changes in an already existing group of working drawings. 2.) The double parlor may have resulted from a specific commission.

Federico Vercelloni was an important textile manufacturer, who apparently wanted "a modern room" for his house in Sordevolo. Unfortunately, members of the Vercelloni family have not permitted further research into the house, so the appearance of the rooms in situ cannot be determined. Details on how Vercelloni and Lauro met or the extent of their relationship are unknown.

45 A memorandum written by a former Wolfson Collection curator and now in the Collection's files links the rooms to a villa in Biella, near Turin. Its author neither identified the owners of the villa nor expounded on whether the rooms had originally been installed as a unit or had appeared in part at the Turin exposition of 1902.

Since further documentation to substantiate the memo's claims about the Biella site may exist, this might still prove a possibility. Yet given the inscription on the case that held the original drawings for the interior and the extensive research conducted in Italy by Mrs. Renata Rutledge, it is safe to assume that these rooms were actually located in Sordevolo.

46 Numerous photographs from the Turin exhibition were given to the Wolfson Collection at the time it acquired the room interior. Beyond establishing the chairs' provenance, the mere presence of the photographs certifies the importance these chairs held in 1902. While the source of these documentary photographs has not been fully identified, they are most likely plates from the book *I Mobili alla Prima Esposizione Internazionale d'Arte Decorativa Moderna.* This extensive volume of individualized plates now serves as a valuable record of the objects and model rooms installed at the Turin exposition of 1902. The separate plates provide crucial documentation of the furniture produced in Italy and the wide variety of the modern qualities achieved.

47 Lauro's official stamp on the bottom of all the double-parlor chairs identifies them as having been produced under his guidance. It may have been a designation of honor that each piece was so labeled.

48 The author of the memorandum discussed in note 45 assumed that the panels, and perhaps the chairs as well, were covered with Liberty and Company brocade, but he failed to designate the exact Liberty models or samples used. Since Lauro employed Italian textile designers to work on his palazzina, he quite possibly relied on these same individuals to create the decorations for the double parlor. This would make it doubtful that these brocades were actually produced by Liberty. Until definitive evidence is found, it is best to consider these brocades as being inspired by Liberty and Company.

49 For further reference to examples of Lauro's furniture at the Turin exposition of 1902, see Alexander Koch, *Erste Internationale Ausstellung für Moderne Dekorative Kunst in Turin,* 225 and 277, with the latter page being most important for the "Speisezimmer," or dining room.

50 It is unclear how the furniture arrangement in each section of the room was intended. The owners may have wanted to be able to move the chairs and tables about freely. This point has not been fully established, since access to the room interiors at Sordevolo, where the pieces were first housed, has so far been denied.

51 Some of this furniture was obviously photographed on the pebbled walkway in front of the palazzina. A sheet was thrown over the stairway to enhance the visual impact of the furniture. This procedure suggests that these pieces either were exhibited in a section of the palazzina which the photographer could not easily reach, or they were displayed in another pavilion, perhaps close to the general Italian section. The actual location of these pieces at Turin has not been precisely established.

52 For further reference, see *I Mobili alla Prima Esposizione.* Also see *L'Architettura alla Prima Esposizione Internazionale d'Arte Decorativa Moderna,* which includes excellent plate reproductions of the major architectural monuments at the exposition.

53 See *Esposizione Nazionale del 1898,* 269. This source precisely describes the "new" Stile Floreale interior the Valabrega firm produced.

54 Fuchs, *Erste Internationale Ausstellung,* 217-24.

55 For further reference to the Valabrega family, see Guttry and Maino, *Il Mobile Liberty Italiano,* 210-20.

56 *Relazione,* 149. This enlightened critique was obviously written with a clear insight into the sources of Cometti's work.

57 For further reference, see Enrico Thovez, "Un Artista Decoratore: Giacomo Cometti," 8-18. Thovez was one of the more influential critics of the period.

Also see Thovez, "L'Arte di Giacomo Cometti," 35-46. Numerous photographs of Cometti's room installations from Turin (1902) appear in this article.

58 Alfredo Melani, "L'Esposizione d'Arte Decorativa Odierna in Torino," (May 1902), 41-42. Melani, a perceptive critic, became the most vociferous supporter of pure modernism. A furniture designer in his own right, Melani's work was rather conservative considering the strength of his written polemics. For further reference, see Rossana Bossaglia, "Ebanisti Italiani d'età Liberty," 154-65.

59 Melani, *ibid.*

60 *Ibid.*

61 Melani, "L'Esposizione d'Arte Decorativa Odierna in Torino," (June 1902), 49-52.

62 *Ibid.*

63 U. Fleres, "Lo Stile Nuovo," 1054-58.

CATALOGUE OF
THE EXHIBITION

1 Vittorio Pica (author)
Book
published by Officine dell'Istituto Italiano
d'Arti Grafiche, Bergamo, Italy
1903
cloth-covered boards with paper
10 1/4 x 7 3/4 x 1 1/8" (26 x 19.7 x 2.9 cm)
title: *L'Arte Decorativa all'Esposizione di
Torino del 1902*

This volume carefully documented the
highlights of each country's presentation
at the 1902 Turin exposition. Pica's even-
handed treatment of decorative design
resulted in this relatively substantial
record of the types of objects and room
ensembles shown there. Today, the volume remains both a critical text and a
solid compendium of photographs of the
designs displayed at Turin.

2 Artist unknown
Postcard
published by Società Editrice Cartoline,
Turin, Italy
1902
chromolithograph
3 1/2 x 5 1/2" (8.9 x 14 cm)
title: *Esposizione Internazionale d'Arte
Decorativa Moderna, Torino 1902,
Palazzina del Comitato col Laghetto*

This postcard offers a view of a lakeside
building constructed for the exposition.
Now a common form of popular art, the
postcard was still a new invention in the
early 1900s.

3 Artist unknown
Postcard
published by Società Editrice Cartoline,
Turin, Italy
1902
chromolithograph
3 1/2 x 5 1/2" (8.9 x 14 cm)
title: *Esposizione Internazionale d'Arte
Decorativa Moderna, Torino 1902,
Vestibolo d'Onore e Facciata Principale*

The main facade of the Hall of Honor was
among the major buildings featured at
the Turin exposition.

4 Artist unknown
Postcard
published by Società Editrice Cartoline,
Turin, Italy
1902
chromolithograph
3 1/2 x 5 1/2" (8.9 x 14 cm)
title: *Esposizione Internazionale d'Arte
Decorativa Moderna, Torino 1902, Edificio
Automobili e Fontane*

By the time of the Turin exposition of
1902, automobiles were entering the
arena of modern design. Implications of
speed, inherent in the automobiles'
forms, fascinated many of the day's
designers.

5 Maurice Biais
Postcard
1902
Turin, Italy
chromolithograph
3 9/16 x 5 1/2" (9.1 x 14 cm)
title: *La Maison Moderne, Salle Principale
de ``La Maison Moderne'' à l'Exposition de
Turin, 1902*

As one of the main private supporters
and entrepreneurs of the art nouveau
period, Julius Meier-Graefe nurtured the
concepts of interior design by allowing
foreign artists to install room ensembles
in his shop and by promoting their
objects as new models of ``advanced''
handicrafts. He was honored, along with
his close friend Siegfried Bing, at the
Turin exposition, although his position
as a design leader even then was being
challenged by others.
   While the furniture in this image may
refer to Meier-Graefe's installation at the
exposition, the postcard's inscription
provides the primary addresses of his
shop in Paris – 82 and 95, rue des Petits-
Champs. The fact that he printed
and circulated a postcard dedicated to
La Maison Moderne demonstrates his
progressive interest in advertising.

6 Leonardo Bistolfi
Postcard
1902
Turin, Italy
chromolithograph
5 1/2 x 3 5/8" (14 x 9.2 cm)
title: *Prima Esposizione Internazionale
d'Arte Decorativa Moderna, Torino, Aprile-
Novembre, 1902*

This fluid design, which corresponds to
those used on the diploma and applied
to wall decorations inside the Italian
pavilion, has become the leitmotif of the
Turin exposition.

7 Leonardo Bistolfi
(with the assistance of Giorentino on
the background design; engraved by
C. Turletti)
Diploma
published by Calcografia G. Gastaldi,
Turin, Italy
1902
engraving
22 7/8 x 31 5/16" (58.1 x 79.5 cm)
title: *Prima Esposizione Internazionale
d'Arte Decorativa Moderna, Torino, 1902*
inscription: J.J. Scharvogel, Ceramista,
Monaco (Baviera)

Like the other awards presented at the
Turin exposition, this diploma depicts
four young women in classical garb hold-
ing a long, flowing scarf. Background
motifs of rambling vines and roses suggest the importance of the cult of nature
and the burgeoning Stile Floreale.

8 Agostino Lauro
Interior rendering: *No 1 Parete Verso
Corridoio* (inner wall to corridor and
lobby)
ca. 1900-01
Italy
watercolor, pencil, and ink on paper
14 x 32" (35.5 x 81.3 cm)
mark: Agostino Lauro / Tappezziere in
Stoffa / Torino (stamped and monogram)
/ '5/6 1901 (in pencil)
second mark: Emanuele Bona / 10121 –
Torino -2 c. so re Umberto (stamped)
watermark: E.V.M.

Crucial to understanding the evolution of
the Sordevolo room interior are these
design renderings. This one shows
Lauro's original "Liberty style" intentions
for wall sections, a corner table, curtains,
and a sofa. Penciled notations and professional names in the borders suggest the
discussions Lauro and others enter-
tained as the room approached actual
production. Today, these drawings exemplify the way Lauro worked to gain his
patrons' approval before final pieces were
constructed.

9 Agostino Lauro
Interior rendering: *No 2 Parete Verso Sala
a Pranzo* (inner wall to the dining room)
ca. 1900-01
Italy
watercolor, pencil, and ink on paper
14 x 22½" (35.5 x 57.1 cm)
mark: Agostino Lauro / Tappezziere in
Stoffa / Torino (stamped and monogram)
/ '5/6 1901 (in pencil)
second mark: Emanuele Bona / 10121
Torino -2 c. so re Umberto (stamped)

Proposed locations for curtains, a vitrine,
and a sofa, clarified by notes and descrip-
tive details penciled in the margins,
appear in this drawing.

10 Agostino Lauro
Interior rendering: *No 3 Verso il Terrazzo
V.F.* (to the balcony)
ca. 1900-01
Italy
watercolor, pencil, and ink on paper
14⅜ x 27" (36.5 x 68.6 cm)
mark: Agostino Lauro / Tappezziere in
Stoffa / Torino (stamped and monogram)
/ '5/6 1901 (in pencil)
second mark: Emanuele Bona / 10121
Torino -2 c. so re Umberto (stamped)
watermark: E.V.M.

Here, interior designs for a "Liberty style"
parlor with wall sections, curtains, and
corner stands are illustrated. Some of
these elements were not included in the
room's final rendering.

11 Agostino Lauro
Interior rendering: *No 4 Parete Verso lo
Studio* (inner wall to studio)
ca. 1900-01
Italy
watercolor, pencil, and ink on paper
14⅜ x 19" (36.5 x 48.3 cm)
mark: Agostino Lauro / Tappezziere in
Stoffa / Torino (stamped and monogram)
/ '5/6 1901 (in pencil)
second mark: Emanuele Bona / 10121
Torino -2 c. so re Umberto (stamped)

Notes in this drawing's margins refer to
designs for a corner table, love seat with
mirror, and doorway.

12 Agostino Lauro
Interior rendering: *No 5 Divisione di
Mezzo* (middle division; divider between
rooms)
ca. 1900-01
Italy
watercolor, pencil, and ink on paper
13¾ x 19" (34.9 x 48.3 cm)

In addition to the designs for an archway
and room dividers, this architectural
sketch displays a center inscription that
mentions the drawing's use as a working
model of the parlor's modifications:
*Disegno del Sig. Ag. Lauro / da /
ritornarsi / dopo che abbia servito per le /
necessarie modificazioni affinchi / il
lavoro possa riuscire per quanto /
possibile come ideato e ordinato / Torino
2 Aprile 1900 / Fed. Vercelloni.*

13 Agostino Lauro
Armchair
ca. 1900-01
Italy
carved mahogany with green silk moiré
fabric
30½ x 23½ x 23" (77.5 x 59.7 x 58.4 cm)

14 Agostino Lauro
Parlor table
ca. 1900-01
Italy
carved mahogany
29½" with 21" diameter (74.9 cm with
53.3 cm diameter)

15 Agostino Lauro
Rectangular table (desk/game table)
ca. 1900-01
Italy
carved mahogany with green velvet inset
31½ x 36½ x 23¾" (80 x 92.7 x 60.3 cm)

16 Agostino Lauro
Sofa
ca. 1900-01
Italy
carved mahogany with green silk moiré
fabric
38¼ x 48¾ x 23" (97.2 x 123.8 x 58.4 cm)

Intended for the double parlor, this piece
exhibits carved chestnut leaves on either
side of the front legs.

17 Agostino Lauro
Love seat
ca. 1900-01
Italy
carved mahogany with green silk moiré fabric
40½ x 47 x 23" (102.9 x 119.4 x 58.4 cm)

18 Agostino Lauro
Corner cabinet
ca. 1900-01
Italy
carved mahogany
109½ x 77 x 45" (278.1 x 195.6 x 114.3 cm)

The chestnut leaf motif that dominates much of the parlor's furniture was actively utilized in this piece.

19 Agostino Lauro
Cabinet (vitrine)
ca. 1900-01
Italy
carved mahogany and beveled glass with brass mounts
87¼ x 43½ x 17¾" (221.6 x 110.5 x 45.1 cm)

This vitrine, one of the room's major pieces, may well have been exhibited at the 1902 Turin exposition. Period photographs certify not only its importance but also the possibility that it was not a unique piece.

20 Agostino Lauro
Side chair
ca. 1900-01
Italy
carved mahogany with green silk moiré fabric
36 x 16½ x 17½" (91.4 x 41.9 x 44.5 cm)

A number of the independent pieces of furniture from this room were displayed at the Turin exposition, either inside the Palazzina Lauro or as part of the Italian pavilion. These models were also available for purchase in slightly different fabric combinations.

21 Agostino Lauro
Mirror
ca. 1900-01
Italy
carved mahogany and mirror
69 x 49¾ x 3¼" (175.3 x 126.4 x 8.3 cm)

The mirror's placement above the love seat and attached to the ceiling's trellis implies that Lauro created this room with a number of prefabricated sections that could be reassembled easily.

22 Agostino Lauro
Corner table
ca. 1900-01
Italy
carved mahogany
32 x 17 x 17" (82 x 43 x 43 cm)

Designed to fit precisely into a corner of the room, this table echoes the motifs of the parlor's architectural elements.

23 Agostino Lauro
Jardinière with tin liner
ca. 1900-01
Italy
carved mahogany with fitted tin liner
11 x 27¼ x 18¾" (28 x 69.2 x 47.6 cm)

24 Ernesto Basile
(with the assistance of sculptor Antonio Ugo and painter Ettore Maria Bergles)
Secretary
produced by Vittorio Ducrot, Palermo, Italy
1903
carved, painted, and gilded mahogany with sculpted, cast-bronze fittings in the form of female nudes, inset leather blotter, and interior door paintings
67 x 44 x 19½" (170.2 x 111.7 x 49.5 cm)

25 Ernesto Basile
Rocking chair
produced by Vittorio Ducrot, Palermo, Italy
ca. 1898-1900
carved maple with woven silk upholstery
32 x 22½ x 46" (81.3 x 57.2 x 116.8 cm)

26 Carlo Bugatti
Library stool or steps
ca. 1902
Italy
walnut, pewter, vellum, and copper
18 x 23¼ x 19¾" (45.7 x 59 x 50.2 cm)

Bugatti often utilized vellum in his creations, as he did in this walnut library stool. An advanced, practical designer, Bugatti regularly combined materials, one indication of his highly experimental nature.

27 Galileo Chini
Tile
produced by l'Arte della Ceramica, Florence, Italy
ca. 1898-99
glazed earthenware
11⅜" square (28.9 cm square)
mark on back:

In Stile Floreale architecture, glazed ceramic tiles with colorful details were used routinely as decorative borders. The presence of natural motifs in curvilinear patterns today represents the initial evolution of the mature Stile Floreale.

28 Galileo Chini
Fireplace surround
produced by l'Arte della Ceramica,
Florence, Italy
ca. 1910
mahogany with glazed earthenware tiles
51 x 56½ x 7¾" (129.6 x 143.5 x 19.7 cm)
mark on reverse of each tile: Same as cat.
no. 27

To this mahogany fireplace mantel and
surround Chini tastefully applied poly-
chrome glazed tiles. The tiles' abstracted
designs and variegated colors further testify to the floral patterns that dominated
the Stile Floreale.

29 Giacomo Cometti
Chair
1902
Italy
carved oak
39¼ x 16⅜ x 14¾" (99.5 x 41.5 x 37.5 cm)

The harmonizing color tones of this
golden oak dining room chair upholstered in a lavender cotton pattern
reflected the delicate qualities of the
international art nouveau movement
Cometti had absorbed.

30 Giacomo Cometti
Table
1902
Italy
carved oak
31⁵⁄₁₆ x 53¾ x 42⅞" (79.5 x 136.5 x 109 cm)

31 Giacomo Cometti
Credenza
1902
Italy
carved oak, brass mounts, and marble
94⅛ x 71⅝ x 24⅝" (239 x 182 x 62.5 cm)

Cometti, one of the most innovative
designers at the Turin exhibition, had
received an honorable mention award at
the Paris Exposition Universelle of 1900,
which signified his stature in the international design community of the time.

32 Alberto Issel
Desk
1902
Italy
oak, metal, leather, fabric, and paint
52³⁄₁₆ x 32⅜ x 19⅜" (132.5 x 82.3 x 49.3
cm)
mark: Alberto / Issel / Genova (stenciled
in white on underside of desk drawer)

Issel's involvement in the Stile Floreale is
evident in the roses and ribbons motif
carved at the top center of this elaborate
oak, drop-front desk.

33 Alberto Issel
Bookcase
1902
Italy
oak with stained and leaded glass and
silver-plated brass mounts
95⅛ x 80⅜ x 17⅜" (241.5 x 204.2 x 44.2
cm)

The sailing vessel motif in stained glass
refers to the shipbuilders who were
among Issel's chief clients. Issel created
motifs that both mirrored his patrons'
interests and allowed him to enliven his
furniture designs.

34 Alberto Issel
Angled sofa
1902
Italy
oak with upholstery
75⅝ x 104 x 27⅜" (192 x 264.2 x 69.5 cm)

A typical English-inspired, high cushion
back permits this piece to fit snugly into
the alcove of a room. This feature inti-
mates that the sofa was considered more
of an architectural detail than a furniture
accessory.

35 Eugenio Quarti
Chair
ca. 1900
Italy
mahogany with mother-of-pearl inlays;
brass, copper, and silver wire; and
upholstery
35½ x 14 x 15" (90.2 x 35.6 x 38.1 cm)

Shown as part of a room installation at
the Paris Exposition Universelle of 1900,
the chair's design indicated that Italian
decorative arts were indeed moving in an
avant-garde direction. It also granted
Quarti a degree of international recognition, which greatly bolstered his reputation in Milan.

36 Eugenio Quarti
Box
ca. 1908-10
Italy
fruitwood with copper, brass, and silver
wire, and mother-of-pearl inlays
3⅜ x 12¾ x 4⅝" (8.6 x 32.4 x 11.8 cm)

This elegantly designed and crafted box,
a late example of the Stile Floreale,
affirms the high level of technical skill
achieved by Italian craftsmen.

37 Vittorio Valabrega
Chair
ca. 1902
Italy
carved walnut with leather and brass
39 x 16½ x 20½" (99 x 42 x 52 cm)

38 Vittorio Valabrega
Table
ca. 1902
Italy
carved walnut
31 7/8 x 52 5/8 x 42 7/8" (79.6 x 133 x 109.5 cm)

A variation of this table and chair (cat. no. 37) with vine and tendril decorations on the feet was exhibited at the Turin exposition. This particular set may have been a model popular with Valabrega's clients.

39 Vittorio Valabrega
Contro-credenza
ca. 1902
Italy
carved walnut with chromed metal mounts, glass, and marble
102 x 68 3/8 x 22 3/4" (259.1 x 173.7 x 57.8 cm)
mark: signed on plaques in four locations, inside the top part of each cabinet door

Sinuous tendrils and vines combined with carved leaves and grape clusters adorn the cabinet's doors. The metalwork on this piece further reinforces the curved accents of the woodwork.

40 Carlo Zen
Curio cabinet
ca. 1902
Italy
mahogany with glass and inlays of brass, mother-of-pearl, and gold leaf
86 5/8 x 40 1/2 x 14 1/4" (220 x 102.8 x 36.2 cm)

Among the more prolific designers and cabinet makers of the period was the firm of Carlo Zen. Some of his decorations suggest the strong influence of continental symbolism, while other objects reveal a keen awareness of geometric simplification.

41 Carlo Zen
Grandfather clock
ca. 1908
Italy
fruitwood with beveled glass and inlays of brass and mother-of-pearl
96 x 21 1/4 x 12 1/4" (243.8 x 54.6 x 31.1 cm)

Even at the end of the first decade of this century, late examples of Stile Floreale still adopted grape cluster and leaf motifs, thus signifying the impact of nature on Italian design.

42 J.H. Gest
Piano and bench
made by Baldwin Piano Company, Cincinnati, Ohio
1904
carved, incised, and painted mahogany
piano: 76 x 57 1/2 x 78" (193 x 146 x 198.1 cm)
bench: 19 1/4 x 37 7/8 x 14 3/4" (48.9 x 96.2 x 37.5 cm)
marks: J.H. Gest 1904 (on lower right of music book holder); Baldwin / Cincinnati / U.S.A. (on label above piano keys)

This ornate work received a first prize at the St. Louis exposition of 1904, one of the primary forums for the arts and crafts movement in the United States. It was displayed in Baldwin piano stores throughout America before a private collector purchased it in 1915.

43 Louis Comfort Tiffany
Vase
ca. 1905
United States
glazed earthenware
8" with 5 1/2" diameter (20.3 cm with 14 cm diameter)
mark:

Tiffany and Company emphasized similar organic qualities in a number of their vases.

44 Designer unknown
Pitcher
manufactured by Gorham Silver Company, New York
1881
sterling silver
9 x 8 1/4" with 7" diameter (22.9 x 20.9 cm with 17.8 cm diameter)
mark on base: Sterling / 1121 / N / Theodore B. Starr / N.Y.

An early penchant for natural designs, particularly cherry blossoms and branches, appears in the fusion of bands of flowers and leaves with traditional decorative motifs.

45 Designer unknown
Container and lid
manufactured by Gorham Silver
Company, New York
ca. 1881
sterling silver and other metals
4¼″ with 3⁹/₁₆″ diameter (10.8 cm with 9
cm diameter)
mark on base: Gorham & Co / Sterling /
& other metals / B2 / N

A craze for Japanese art swept the United
States after the Philadelphia Centennial
exposition in 1876, where actual Japanese crafts and prints were displayed.
American investigations into natural
motifs thus received additional attention,
since Japanese art advocated a similar
``cult of nature'' approach to design.
Here, pea pods, ferns, vines, a spider and
its web, and a bird on a cherry blossom
branch intimate the delicacy of Japanese
decorations.

46 W.A.S. Benson
Firescreen
1891
England
copper and brass
25 x 20½″ x 7¹³/₁₆″ (63 x 52.1 x 19.9 cm)
mark: REGˢ Nº / 181515

The form of a sunflower – the symbol of
the aesthetic movement in Great Britain –
provided a motif for this firescreen with
an adjustable base and angled copper
blades (an extremely ingenious design
for 1891). Benson, a leader in the English
arts and crafts tradition, encouraged his
craftsmen to produce such practical
designs in metal. Well received on the
continent, Benson's metalwork pieces
were carried by Siegfried Bing's shop,
L'Art Nouveau, in Paris from 1895-96 on.

47 Thomas Jeckyll
Fireplace surround
manufactured by Barnard, Bishop and
Barnard, Norwich, England
1873
cast iron with silvered bronze patina
36 x 36³/₈ x 1³/₄″ (91.5 x 92.4 x 4.4 cm)
mark: three concentric letter Bs

Jeckyll has often been mentioned with
the American artist James Abbott McNeill
Whistler as an early designer active in the
modernization of room interiors. Inspired
by Japanese art, Jeckyll integrated natural motifs, such as sunflowers, butterflies,
and dragonflies, with abstract designs
derived from Japanese crests.

48 William Morris
Wallpaper sample
produced by William Morris and
Company
designed 1873; manufactured ca. 1880
England
printed paper
23 x 21⅛″ (58.4 x 53.6 cm)

The early date of this wallpaper's design
and manufacture documents the well-
established British interest in using
motifs from nature. Wallpapers with floral
patterns, like these lilies, marigolds,
and bluebonnets on a leafy ground, provided another opportunity for nature to
enter a room interior.

49 William Morris
Wallpaper sample
produced by William Morris and
Company
ca. 1900
England
printed paper
23⅞ x 22″ (60.7 x 55.9 cm)

50 William Morris
Wallpaper sample
produced by William Morris and
Company
ca. 1900
England
printed paper
23 x 22″ (58.5 x 55.9 cm)

This honeysuckle pattern as well as the
poppy design (cat. no. 51) proved quite
popular with Morris and Company
clientele.

51 William Morris
Wallpaper sample
produced by William Morris and
Company
ca. 1900
England
printed paper
23 x 22″ (58.5 x 55.9 cm)

52 William Morris
Wallpaper sample
produced by William Morris and
Company
ca. 1900
England
printed paper
18³/₄ x 21⅞″ (47.5 x 55.5 cm)

Another turn-of-the-century reference
to the use of flowers and nature as wall
ornamentation was this garden tulip
pattern.

53 Charles Voysey
Curtain panel
woven for Liberty and Company, London,
England by Alexander Morton and Company, Kilmarnock, Scotland
ca. 1897
cotton
30½ x 33½″ (77.5 x 85.1 cm)

Voysey incorporated this fabric into the
W. Ward Higgs residence, located at 23
Queensborough Terrace, Bayswater,
London, when he designed the house's
interior in the late 1890s.

54 Designer unknown
Tile
produced by Mintons China Works,
Stoke-on-Trent, England
ca. 1880
glazed earthenware
8" square (20.3 cm square)
mark:

A stenciled design of fruit and branches
fills the tile's surface.

55 Designer unknown
Electric heater
ca. 1905
Scotland
hammered and pierced copper,
and cast iron
29¾ x 14 x 11¾" (75.6 x 35.5 x 29.8 cm)

This electric heater with a pierced floral
design on its circular top also includes a
stylized tree motif, which suggests that
derivations from the Glasgow School
were occasionally employed.

56 V.C. Andreoli
Design for a vase: Indian cress
for the Rozenburg Factory, the Hague,
Holland
ca. 1900
watercolor and pencil on paper
10⅞ x 8¼" (27.6 x 21 cm)

mark: Andreoli (in pencil)

Motifs of Indian cress and morning glo-
ries accentuate the shape of the vase.

57 Attributed to V.C. Andreoli
Design for a vase: crab motif
for the Rozenburg Factory, the Hague,
Holland
ca. 1900
watercolor and pencil on paper
13¾ x 13" (35 x 33.1 cm)

The cult of nature was not limited to an
appreciation of flowers, tendrils, and
vines. Designers, as here, freely turned to
sea or land animals for elements of their
compositions. Japanese *ukiyo-e* prints,
which often displayed such strong visual
forms as this crab motif, may have
inspired this tendency.

58 J. Barendsen
Design for a vase: tulips
for the Rozenburg Factory, the Hague,
Holland
ca. 1905
watercolor and pencil on paper
9⅛ x 6¼" (23.1 x 15.9 cm)
mark: J. Barendsen (in pencil)

59 Attributed to S. Schellink
Design for a tableau of sixty-six tiles with
water lilies
for the Rozenburg Factory, the Hague,
Holland
ca. 1897
watercolor and pencil on paper
19⅛ x 11" (48.5 x 28 cm)

60 Attributed to S. Schellink
Design for a tableau of eleven tiles with
chrysanthemums
for the Rozenburg Factory, the Hague,
Holland
ca. 1897
watercolor and pencil on paper
11⅞ x 4¹⁵⁄₁₆" (30.2 x 12.5 cm)

61 Attributed to J.W. van Rossum
Design for a tableau of eighty-four tiles
with bulbs/flowers
for the Rozenburg Factory, the Hague,
Holland
ca. 1897
watercolor and pencil on paper
10 x 13⅜" (25.4 x 33.9 cm)

During the late 1890s and early 1900s,
ceramic tiles, installed as room friezes,
were often used to enliven apartments
and villas.

62 School of Peter Behrens
Plate
produced by Krautheim & Adelberg,
Selb, Bavaria
1902
Germany
porcelain
12½" diameter (31.7 cm diameter)
mark:

To maintain control over distribution to a
select clientele, Behrens sold a limited
number of pieces through a special shop
he organized in Nuremberg. Only designs
approved by the Bayerisches Gewerbe
Museum (Bavarian Trade Museum) in
Nuremberg received the mark shown
above. The number on the piece – 3859 –
might refer to the model number in the
firm's design book, not to the plate's decorative pattern.

63 Peter Behrens
Plate
produced by Porzellanfabrik Gebrüder
Bauscher, Weiden, Germany
1901
porcelain
9½″ diameter (24.8 cm diameter)
mark:

Behrens designed this dinner service,
with its advanced application of abstract
natural motifs, for use in his own dining
room on the Mathildenhöhe in
Darmstadt.

64 Otto Eckmann
Tile
produced by Villeroy and Boch
Mosaikfabrik, Mettlach, Germany
ca. 1900
glazed earthenware
5¾″ square (14.6 cm square)
impressed mark on back: Villeroy and
Boch / Mosaikfabrik / in / Mettlach / H L

The design on this glazed tile can be considered a variation of Jugendstil motifs.
Its geometric abstractions reveal
Germany's sympathy towards the avant-
garde Jugendstil, an awareness displayed much earlier there than in most
countries involved in the art nouveau
movement.

65 Max Laeuger
Vase
manufactured by Tonwerke Kandern,
Germany
1905
glazed earthenware with gold mosaic
inlays
10¼ x 6¼″ (26 x 15.9 cm)
mark:

A heavily stylized decoration inspired by
vines encircles this vase.

66 Designer unknown
Tile
produced by Osterather Mosaik und
Wandplattenfabrik, Osterath nr.
Düsseldorf, Germany
ca. 1902
glazed earthenware
5⅞″ square (14.9 cm square)

This tile and one created by Otto
Eckmann (cat. no. 64) exemplify a
Jugendstil variety of continental art
nouveau.

67 Designer unknown
Tile
produced by Osterather Mosaik und
Wandplattenfabrik, Osterath nr.
Düsseldorf, Germany
ca. 1902
glazed earthenware
5⅞″ square (14.9 cm square)

68 Theo Schmuz-Baudiss
Vase
produced by Königliche Porzellan
Manufaktur, Berlin, Germany
ca. 1895-1900
porcelain
4⅞″ with 5½″ diameter (12.4 cm with 14
cm diameter)
mark:

One way by which designers imagina-
tively transformed organic shapes appropriate to the cult of nature is suggested in
the floral elements of this squat vase.

69 Ferdinand Selle
Plate
produced for Porzellan Manufaktur-
Burgau, Thüringia, Germany/Austria
ca. 1907
glazed earthenware
11¼″ diameter (28.6 cm diameter)
mark:

70 Designer unknown
Tile
produced by Wessel's Wandplatten-
Fabrik, Bonn, Germany
ca. 1902
glazed earthenware
5⅝″ square (14.3 cm square)
mark:

Highly reminiscent of Jugendstil tendencies is the raised relief on this ceramic tile.

71 Hector Guimard
Jardinière
produced by Manufacture Nationale de
Porcelaine, Sèvres, France
ca. 1907
soft-paste porcelain
8″ with 13″ diameter (20.3 cm with 33 cm
diameter)
mark on base:

After 1900 Guimard worked at Sèvres,
where he became adept at producing
designs realized in porcelain. These
objects, including this jardinière,
employed some naturalistic motifs but for
the most part were based upon
Guimard's interpretation of nature's
organic qualities.

72 Henry van de Velde
Coffeepot and lid
produced by Staatliche Porzellan
Manufaktur, Meissen, Germany
ca. 1905
porcelain
6³⁄₈″ with 3¹⁄₂″ diameter (16.2 cm with 8.9
cm diameter)
mark:

During the mid-1890s, van de Velde was
recognized as one of the moving forces
behind art nouveau design in Belgium.
His room ensembles, both for Siegfried
Bing at *L'Art Nouveau* and for Julius
Meier-Graefe at *La Maison Moderne*,
ranked among the decade's more progressive efforts in interior design.
   Working in all media, including tapes-
try, van de Velde gradually freed himself
from painting to concentrate on design
and architecture.

73 Henry van de Velde
Sugar bowl and lid
produced by Staatliche Porzellan
Manufaktur, Meissen, Germany
ca. 1905
porcelain
3³⁄₈ x 5⁵⁄₈ x 5″ (8.6 x 14.3 x 12.7 cm)

Van de Velde's abstract designs on these
porcelain pieces were anticipated by
some of his work of the late 1890s.

BIBLIOGRAPHY

Aitelli, Efisto. "Esposizione Internazionale d'Arte Decorativa Moderna in Torino: L'Italia, gl'Italiani." *Natura ed Arte* (1 November 1902): 750-62.

Bossaglia, Rossana. *Il Liberty in Italia*. Milan, 1968.

_____ . "Ebanisti Italiani d'età Liberty." *Kalos* 1 (1970): 3-14.

_____ . *Liberty in Italy*. Florence, 1978.

Brosio, Valentino. *Lo Stile Liberty in Italia*. Milan, 1967.

Catalogo della Prima Esposizione Internazionale d'Arte Decorativa Moderna. Turin, 1902.

Crane, Walter. "Modern Decorative Art at Turin: General Impressions." *Magazine of Art* (1902): 488-93.

Cremona, Italo. *Il Tempo dell'Art Nouveau*. Florence, 1964.

Esposizione Nazionale del 1898. Turin, 1898.

Fierens-Gevaert, H. "L'Esposition de Turin." *Revue de l'Art Ancien et Moderne* (July-December 1902): 65ff.

Fleres, U. "Lo Stile Nuovo." *Rivista d'Italia* 2, year 5, no. 12: 1054-58.

Fratini, Francesca R. *Esposizione Torino 1902, Polemiche in Italia sull'Arte Nuova*. Turin, 1903. Reprint, 1970.

Fred, W. "Die Turiner Ausstellung." *Die Kunst* 6 (1902).

_____ . "The International Exhibition of Decorative Art at Turin: The Italian Section." *International Studio* 17 (July-October 1902): 273-79.

Frizzi, A. "L'Esposizione Internazionale d'Arte Decorativa Moderna a Torino, 1902: La Villa Lauro." *L'Ingegneria Civile e le Arti Industriali*. Turin, 1902.

Fuchs, Georg. "Italian Applied Arts at the Turin Exhibition, 1902." *Erste Internationale Ausstellung für Moderne Dekorative Kunst in Turin*. Darmstadt, 1903.

_____ . "L'Art industriel italien à l'Exposition de Turin, 1902." In "L'Exposition internationale des arts décoratifs modernes à Turin, Mai-Octobre 1902." *Deutsche Kunst und Dekoration* 1 (1902-3): 217-42.

Guida alla Prima Esposizione Internazionale d'Arte Decorativa Moderna, 1902. Turin, 1902.

Guttry, Irene de, and Maria Paola Maino. *Il Mobile Liberty Italiano*. Roma-Bari, 1983.

I Mobili alla Prima Esposizione Internazionale d'Arte Decorativa Moderna. Vol. 1. Turin, 1902.

Koch, Alexander. "Das Italienische Kunst-Gewerbe auf der Turiner Ausstellung 1902." *Erste Internationale Ausstellung für Moderne Dekorative Kunst in Turin*. Darmstadt, 1903.

L'Architettura alla Prima Esposizione Internazionale d'Arte Decorativa Moderna. Turin, 1902.

Madsen, S. Tschudi. *Sources of Art Nouveau*. New York, 1975.

Marx, Roger. "L'Exposition internationale d'art dècoratif moderne á Turin." *Gazette des Beaux-Arts* 28 (December 1902): 506-10.

Meeks, Carroll L.V. "The Real 'Liberty' of Italy: The Stile Floreale." *Art Bulletin* (June 1961): 113-30.

Melani, Alfredo. "L'Art Nouveau at Turin. An Account of the Exposition by A. Melani and a Member of the International Committee of Direction." *The Architectural Record* 12, no. 6 (November 1902): 585-99.

_____ . "L'Art Nouveau at Turin. A Description of the Exhibition by A. Melani, a Member of the International Jury." *The Architectural Record* 12, no. 7 (December 1902): 735-50.

_____ . "L'Esposizione d'Arte Decorativa Odierna in Torino." *Arte Italiana Decorativa ed Industriale* 3, no. 5 (May 1902): 41-42; no. 6 (June 1902): 49-52.

Pantini, Romualdo. "L'Esposizione di Torino: gl'Italiani." *Il Marzocco* 7, no. 32 (10 August 1902): 2.

Pica, Vittorio. *L'Arte Decorativa all'Esposizione di Torino del 1902*. Bergamo, 1903.

Pistoi, Mila Leva. *Torino Mezzo Secolo di Architettura, 1865-1915*. Turin, 1969.

Puglia, Raffaella del. *Mobili a Ambienti Italiani dal Gotico al Floreale*. Milan, 1963.

Relazione della Giuria Internazionale della Prima Esposizione d'Arte Decorativa Moderna. Vol. 1. Turin, 1902.

Rembrandt, Carlo. *Ettore Jean Bugatti*. Rizzoli, 1982.

Soulier, Gustave. "Exposition internationale d'art dècoratif moderne á Turin." *L'Art Dècoratif* (June 1902): 129-30.

Thovez, Enrico. "Cronaca dell'Esposizione Internazionale d'Arte Decorativa Moderna a Torino." *L'Arte Decorativa Moderna* (January 1902): 1-3.

_____ . "The First International Exhibition of Modern Decorative Art at Turin." *International Studio* 17 (July-October 1902): 45-47.

_____ . "The International Exhibition of Modern Decorative Art at Turin: The Dutch Section." *International Studio* 17 (July-October 1902): 204ff.

_____ . "The Turin Exhibition: The Belgian Section." *International Studio* 17 (July-October 1902): 279ff.

_____ . "Un Artista Decoratore: Giacomo Cometti." *L'Arte Decorativa Moderna* year 2, no. 6: 8-18.

_____ . "L'Arte di Giacomo Cometti." *L'Artista Moderno* 12 (1903): 35-46.

Weisberg, Gabriel P. *Art Nouveau Bing: Paris Style 1900*. New York, 1986.

INDEX